Sidelines and Stilettos

A GIRL'S GUIDE TO TALKING SPORTS

BY

Kristy Hendley McGhee

ISBN-13: 978-1-935256-03-8

Contact us at:
ledgepress@gmail.com
L' Edge Press
P.O. Box 1652
Boone, NC 28607

Graphic Design:
Abbie Frease
abbie.frease@gmail.com
www.abbiefrease.com

to
mom and dad

for fostering in me
the love of the girlie,
the love of the game,
and
the Love.

grateful.

most.

ABOUT THE AUTHOR:

Kristy Hendley McGhee grew up with four brothers and had no choice but to be around the world of sports and the language of sports. One of her granddads played for the Pittsburgh Steelers. Her brothers played different sports (one even plays pro basketball in Europe) and one of her brothers is a car fanatic (fixes, races and all around brilliant about most things). Several of her uncles are scratch golfers. One of her cousins plays on the PGA Tour and won the 2009 US Open. So you see, Kristy was immersed in sports.

But her ability to speak the language of sports is all her doing. She speaks "sports" because she has read, watched and listened. She has a grasp of a male dominated language and she has the unique ability to help girls (and yes, even guys) to better comprehend and speak this language.

Kristy is my daughter. She is all girl and knows more about a given sport than I ever will. And I have played sports all my life (but I am not a scratch golfer).

Several years ago I challenged Kristy to write a book. "About what?" she asked. "It does not matter," I replied. "Write about something you enjoy and others would want to read. You have a way with words, and you can stop a thought with your words." So, she did.

I have asked each of my kids to write a book. To tell their stories. Why? Because I believe that each of them have something to tell this world. This is Kristy's first book. And guess what? Her brothers are following in her footsteps. Stay tuned.

Kristy's Dad

THE MOTIVATION
(ERRR...ACKNOWLEDGEMENTS):

Clearly, many people had a part in making this little book come to life. (Someone had to listen to my stories!) And I'd like to thank them. So deal with it. And I mean that in the nicest way possible, sugar!

Several friends lived many of these stories with me as they happened. "The Team" – made up of Amy, Casey and Steve – witnessed many of these events, or heard about them as soon as they took place. They also provided countless hours of entertaining sports commentary. Ever the peanut gallery. "The Get Along Gang" – made up of Flowe, Ravelli, Kendra, Ben, Vance and Sam Ed among others – were witnesses, a sounding board and the ultimate tailgate companions.

The group of girls that asked me about sports, heard these stories after the fact, and finally convinced me to put the words in my head onto paper deserve heaps of credit – Abbie, Allison, Brandi, Davis and Emily. Thank you. Abbie deserves credit for the title. (She's also the graphic designer for this little project and available for freelance work. Hire her, people.)

And, of course, I need to thank my ridiculously amazing family – mom, dad, brothers and their wives (Libbi, Jeff, Dickson, Amber, Beattie, Todd, Bo, Billy, and Heather). Whew! A mouthful. They have the tremendous ability to make everything a little bit more competitive and a lot more fun. Even loving each other. Plus one.

That is all.

Kristy

THE BEGINNING:

"You are going to make some guy very happy one day!"

"He is one lucky man!"

"You're like one of the guys but better...a skirt and stilettos!"

"Dude, she's awesome!"

I've heard it all. And not just recently. Comments about how lucky a guy is to have me on his arm have been tossed my direction since high school. Now, before you go and get all huffy about it, it's not what you think. I'm not that girl. Not that girl at all. These comments don't have anything to do with being eye candy or an arm trophy. But, boy oh boy, do I have everyone fooled! This phenomenon is based solely upon tidbits of knowledge about one topic that I've gleaned through the years. Sports.

A girl in a skirt and stilettos who can carry her weight in a conversation about sports. Novel idea, right? Women can vote, climb the corporate ladder, break stereotypes, grow other humans inside their bellies, and become better than ever. But a lady who can enter into any room and bring something relevant to a conversation about sports? That's seemingly unheard of. And apparently a very impressive feat. Welcome to my world.

It all started back in fifth grade. My family settled in North Carolina after moving around a lot. March of fifth grade is a tough time to land at a new school in a new state. The much anticipated middle school, complete with bells to change class, braces, glasses, big bangs and bad perms, was just around the corner.

My soon to be new best friend Carmen immediately took me under her wing. "Who do you like?" she asked, eyes wide with anticipation. Sensing our soon to be new best friend-ness I answered honestly, "Danny in the front is really cute."

Carmen looked at me like I had grown a second head or a third eye or something equally outlandish. "Nooooo," she replied in disbelief. "Who do you like in basketball? Duh! It's almost the ACC Tournament!"

And so it began. In 5th grade.

Until that point, I had been exposed only to football. My brother (the first of four to grace me with his presence), cousins and I would all be herded into the back of any number of wood paneled station wagons and driven to Clemson football games. But it was never about the game. It was about sitting in the back of the station wagon in the seats that faced backwards and eating the fried chicken meant for tailgating while trying not to throw up. (Lucas failed at that. But to this day he claims the chicken was green.) It was about rolling down the big grassy hill. It was about yelling at the top of our lungs for no other reason than 60,000 other people were doing it too and not getting in trouble for it. It was about learning that, for some reason, we were supposed to hate (or "strongly dislike" as explained by mom, because we're not allowed to hate anyone) the University of South Carolina.

We lived outside of Chicago when I was in second through fourth grades. It was there that my interest in football became personal. The 1985 Chicago Bears won Super Bowl XX. (They actually played and won the game in January of 1986. Just one of those things. Kind of like A, E, I, O, U and sometimes Y.) And I lived there! How could I not be excited? The entire city was on a manic high! They even had a song called "The Super Bowl Shuffle" that was played on every local radio station. (Think really big boy band meets really awful rap group minus any dancing talent). And then there was my first true love. The quarterback of the team, one Mr. Jim McMahon (a.k.a. the "Punky QB" as he so eloquently referred to himself). My dad would lift me up to kiss the face of his life size poster every night before bed.

But these instances were menial compared to what happened when we moved to North Carolina. I was being asked for my opinion about sports for the first time. And the stage was set.

Just so you understand, the city of Greensboro, NC, is a hub of college basketball activity even without the presence of a major division I (D1) university. It is close enough to NC State (simply State), Duke, University of North Carolina (simply UNC or Carolina) and Wake Forest (Wake) to be a home to fans from each school. These schools are distinctly known as "Tobacco Road" in college basketball circles because the first three are located within 27 miles of one another in a state where the historical cash crop is tobacco. They are about an hour east of Greensboro, while Wake is about 30 minutes west. And, Greensboro had the distinct honor of hosting the ACC (Atlantic Coast Conference) Tournament for men's basketball for many years. These things allowed a passion for college basketball to reach a frenzy come tournament time. Luckily, those unfortunate souls who actually had to be in school on the Friday of the tournament were allowed to watch the games on TV. (As a standing rule, every TV in every classroom in Greensboro is turned on for the basketball games on that day.)

Soon to be new best friend – Carmen – was including me in life as she knew it. It was my job, my mission as the new kid trying to fit in, to form an intelligent opinion. My social standing depended upon it. Carmen had quickly announced her allegiance to Carolina, noting that the majority of the class held the same opinion. The other major group cheered for NC State, while a few liked Wake and hardly anyone pulled for Duke. (Carolina is the dreaded enemy of both Duke and State. Think Communist Russia to the USA during the Cold War.) With all of my fifth grade wisdom, I spent that afternoon and evening determined to make my own decision about which team to cheer for. I longed to sound knowledgeable about this new topic of basketball with my new friends, so I scoured the pages of the sports section of the local newspaper and Sports Illustrated. (ACC men's basketball is such a big deal that Sports Illustrated devotes a significant amount of time, resources and pages in the magazine in order that the entire nation may be exposed to what those of us in the area get on a daily basis.)

After several hours of research, I had come to an independent, intelligent decision. The team that I would pledge my allegiance to was…drum roll, please…Duke! GASP! (I know what you're thinking. How could Carmen and I ever become new best friends since I was choosing to pull for the USA over her Communist Russia? Wonders never cease.) To this day, I maintain that my choice was informed and thorough. The research had clearly shown that Duke had the cutest players. And that was that.

What began as a simple question and a bit of interest – complete with decisions made for all the wrong reasons – has turned into a hobby and interest for me. Sports. Okay, well maybe it's more along the lines of a passion and obsession. But you see where I'm going. If a ten year old girl can have opinions about sports, then anyone can. What you'll find in the pages that follow are guidelines for forming your own opinion. You don't have to know every detail about every sport. I sure don't. It's not worth it. Actually, I just don't care about all of them enough to bother. If you form educated opinions and tuck away a few nuggets about one or two sports, then you will have conversation pieces to last a lifetime.

Sports are the lowest common denominator in our culture. The average man has an opinion one way or the other about sports. And that, my dear, sets you up perfectly.

You know how flattering it is when a man notices your (insert latest girly thing here – haircut, hair color, skirt, stilettos, pocket book). He doesn't pretend to know everything about that topic, which is fine because that would just be weird. What we all love is that he noticed. He took interest. He mentioned it in conversation. Imagine how he will feel when the tables are turned and you can offer that same interest, those same pieces of conversation about things in his world. You, dear lady, will make him a very happy man!

THE RULES:

1. **It isn't necessary to learn everything about every sport.** That takes far too much time. Choose the one or two sports that actually interest you the most for whatever reasons (cutest guys, shortest season, fewest players, best uniforms etc.). Learning about them will be much easier that way. The goal is not to know as much as or more than the average male sports fan. The goal is to be able to understand, to a reasonable extent, what's being said about a game and to be able to have a conversation about the team or sport(s) that you choose.

2. **Choose your allegiances wisely.**

    a. It is always acceptable to choose to cheer for a team that you have ties to. Regarding college athletics, you can be a fan of the team where you went to school or where family members went to school. It is usually acceptable to be a fan of a collegiate team in your home state or local area. Typically, people choose to cheer for professional sports teams to which they have personal ties. Those ties can come in the form of location, hometown, favorite college players on the team, etc. When choosing to be a new fan of a team that is doing particularly well in a given sport, be prepared to be called a "bandwagon fan." Other sports fans may look down on you for cheering for the team that is doing well. They will insist that you just jumped on the bandwagon. This is not a compliment. You either have to back up your choice with the reason you chose to cheer for the team or admit that you are, indeed, a bandwagon fan. Admitting it with a laugh and a smile can go a long way in diffusing hard feelings.

b. It is also acceptable to cheer for a team that is the arch rival of a team that you hate – or any team that is playing the team you hate. If accused of being a bandwagon fan in this instance, simply say that you hate the other team. So, clearly, you want their rival to win.

c. It is always acceptable to cheer for the underdog.

3. **Having one or two sports trivia questions that you know the answer to can go a long way.** These typically end up being similar to party tricks and get guys talking about the question you asked. The fact that you know the answer is a good thing.

4. **Don't talk sports all the time.** It will get on everyone's nerves. Having a few conversational topics about sports in your arsenal insures that you are well rounded and that you always have something to discuss with the guys.

5. **It's okay to ask him intelligent questions about the game.** Just don't do it during the action. Wait until a timeout, a commercial or after the game. However, it is perfectly fine to yell at the TV, the coaches, players and officials during the action.

6. **He will appreciate your effort.** If you have hated sports or nagged guys for their passion/obsession with a game, team, Sports Center, he will love that you can actually watch sports on TV with him. He will be impressed when you can speak intelligently about sports. And know that you don't have to agree with him or cheer for the same teams! The friendly rivalry and occasional wager can be fun! His friends will be jealous that he has you on his arm.

THE FAVORITES...WELL, MINE ANYWAY:

College Basketball:

As you are well aware, my original allegiance was with Duke. While I am not as passionate about them as I once was, I remain interested in them and cheer for them unless they are playing for a team that I care about more. I went to graduate school at NC State and work there now (for the Alumni Association – join people...alumni, fans, friends, fans of friends, friends of fans are all welcome), so they have my heart. One of my brothers played college basketball at Wake Forest before transferring to University of North Carolina at Wilmington to play ball. (That brother now plays professionally in Europe.) I still cheer for Wake, unless they are playing State, and I am a UNCW fan.

I also tend to cheer for the underdog in any game that doesn't involve one of the above teams.

I despise the University of North Carolina. I have often said I would cheer for communist Russia over the Tar Heels. I have a good friend, Flowe, whose father actually snuck into a UNC exhibition game against Russia in the early 70's and cheered openly for America's enemy. As a State student, he chose to cheer for the enemy of America rather than the enemy of NC State. I love that man.

National Basketball Association – NBA:

I am a Dallas Mavericks fan because I like Dirk Nowitzski. I liked Dirk even more when Steve Nash played with him. But sadly, Nash had to leave to go play for the Phoenix Suns. I can't say that was a bad choice for him. He's been enormously successful there. But I did so enjoy Nash and Nowitzski as a dynamic duo.

My favorite NBA player of all time is Pete Maravich. The man was an icon. My favorite professional basketball player is my brother Todd. He plays in Europe.

I tend to follow several individual players who I watched in college or have had a chance to meet over the years, but I don't avidly watch their teams every chance I get.

I will choose a team to follow in the playoffs and finals just for something to do.

College Football:

Again, since I am an alumnus and employee of NC State, I am an avid State fan. This has been the case since we moved to North Carolina in 5th grade. My dad got season tickets to State games through work. So I have been going to State games and cheering for them since then. Because my granddad and several family members went to Clemson and played football there, I also cheer for the Tigers. When State plays Clemson, I choose State.

I hate Ohio State. When Philip Rivers, one of NC State's greatest quarterbacks, was a senior, we (State) traveled to play Ohio State. Ohio State is always a strong team. But there was something magical about NC State that year. There was talk of a Heisman Trophy for Philip Rivers, even mumblings of a national championship if we could get past Ohio State with a win. The game went into triple overtime. And we lost. It was a heartbreaking loss and I will forever root against Ohio State.

My favorite college football player right now is Tim Tebow. The kid is a monster quarterback for the University of Florida (having just graduated from the University of Florida). But, aside from being arguably one of the greatest college quarterbacks, nay college football players of all time, I admire and respect him for his values and character. He leads by example. I like that.

National Football League – NFL:

I love the Pittsburgh Steelers. My granddad played for them back in the day. And I mean way back in the day. So therein lays my connection. I love them unabashedly. I have a jersey. I wear it.

I follow the Carolina Panthers because they are the "local" team. And there are certain players on a myriad of teams that I cheer for just because. As bandwagon as it sounds, Peyton Manning is one of those. And he has really funny commercials.

My favorite NFL player is Troy Polamalu. He is a safety and plays for the Steelers. The man is defense incarnate. It's almost like he and the football have a magnetic force. Wherever the football is, there you will find one Mr. Troy Polamalu.

Major League Baseball – MLB:

I cheer for the Atlanta Braves because they are the closest thing we have to a local team. But, what is stronger than that is my dislike of the New York Yankees. My feelings for the Yankees approach the level of my feelings of UNC. Because of my aversion to the Yankees, I cheer openly for the Boston Red Sox, their arch rival. I have no good reason for why I don't like the Yankees. None at all.

I will cheer for the Cubs if they are around for the playoffs because they are the consummate underdog. It's about time that team wins the World Series.

Like with the NBA, I will choose a team to cheer for in the playoffs and World Series just for something to do.

National Hockey League – NHL:

I am a Carolina Hurricanes fan because they are the local team. Truth be told, while I have always enjoyed watching any sporting event in person, I didn't start to care for the Hurricanes until they made a run for the Stanley Cup in 2002. Sadly, they lost. But, in their successful run for the Stanley Cup in 2006, I followed very closely and cheered very loudly. I was such a fan. Even though they are the local team, it is safe to say that there were some bandwagon tendencies in my allegiance.

Golf:

Lucas Glover, a Clemson graduate, is my favorite golfer. The kid is good! And he's family. But I would love him even if we weren't related! I also tend to cheer for Phil ("Lefty") Mickelson because of his underdog status as compared to Tiger Woods. As much as I respect Tiger Woods (this has changed due to the latest reports about Woods) for his skill and dominance in golf, I choose to cheer for the field over Tiger every time. Tiger seems to win all the time. I like it when the other guys have a chance to win, too. I also loved the late great Payne Stewart for his knickers and his character.

NASCAR:

I like Tony Stewart because I find him entertaining. That's about it. The man has road rage at times and is very candid about it. I find that refreshing. Who wouldn't have road rage after driving in circles in heavy traffic for hundreds of miles? I enjoy Kasey Khane because he's dreamy.

Surfing:

Yes, I have a favorite professional surfer. His name is Dave Yearwood. Who cares that I know nothing about surfing? And so what if I've never seen him surf? He's still my favorite because he's pretty much an extra brother. (See? You can choose your favorites for any reason at all!) As an added bonus, his wife owns my FAVORITE little boutique in Wrightsville Beach, NC. Hallelu. Seriously, my closet looks like Hallelu threw up in it. Check out the shop, ladies. You won't be sad you did. And guys, get a little something for your girl there. She'll be super excited!

THE CHANNEL
(ESPN - THE WORLDWIDE LEADER):

It's quite impressive to mention ESPN in a conversation with guys. I met a guy I'll call Password Guy (more details later) through some mutual friends at a dinner party. We really hit it off and talked the entire evening. At some point during the hours of conversation, PG and I discovered that we both had an intense love for the Pittsburgh Steelers. He was pleasantly surprised that I was able to have an intelligent conversation about the Steelers and football, in general. I even threw in an ESPN reference at some point in the evening. A first date was inevitable. I mean, I was wearing a really great pink skirt and a killer pair of black stilettos, after all. That the date would be so soon after meeting, I solely credit to the mutual love of the Steelers and my offhanded comment about ESPN.

PG came to pick me up for the always nerve wracking first date. He knocked on the door and looked cuter than ever. I was almost ready. Really. I only needed a minute or two more. (Those two minutes are always mysterious. I'm sure guys wonder just what the heck we're doing since we don't look any different from when we opened the door two minutes earlier.) During my finishing touches, PG made himself at home. I liked that. He sat down on the sofa and promptly turned on the TV. And what channel immediately popped up? None other than ESPN. That TV had a way of turning on to the channel that was on last when it was turned off. And since I had been watching SportsCenter while I put my makeup on a bit earlier, ESPN was the first thing PG saw when he turned on the TV.

I will never forget the look on the boy's face. I walked into the room and told him I was ready to go. He had the remote in his hand and his jaw dropped. I felt pretty. Which made me confident. And confidence is everything. But, in all honesty, I don't think he noticed any of this. His jaw had dropped when he turned on the TV and saw ESPN. The fact that I looked cute may or may not have added to the moment. After he pulled himself together, PG told me that he knew I liked sports because we talked about it some during our marathon conversation the night we met. But, it knocked his socks off to know that I actually watched ESPN. Who knew I had that kind of power?

I had a great time with PG. It was very convenient that we both liked sports and loved the Steelers. Actually, he loved sports. He took loving sports to a whole new level. I learned a lot from him. Some of the best times we had together involved doing a whole lot of nothing and watching some game on TV.

It was so fun to surprise him. I knew the Steelers were coming to North Carolina to play the Panthers, so I snagged us a couple of tickets for the game in Charlotte. He was so excited! And so was I. Wearing my Steelers jersey but still looking ever so girlie, I got to watch my favorite team live on the field while sitting next to a really cute guy. Plus, I got to eat a stadium hot dog. (I won't get started on stadium hot dogs. But know this: a hot dog from any stadium in America will always be delicious. Always.) Sometimes life is just that good.

A few weeks before the game in Charlotte, after we had only gone out a couple of times, PG and I had "the talk" that took our relationship to a whole new level. Well, probably not the talk you're thinking about. Nonetheless, the talk confirmed PG's feelings for me. It confirmed the respect he had for me, my thoughts, and my opinions. It was the fantasy football talk. PG had been in a fantasy football league with several buddies for years. It was a very big deal. They all spent a weekend in Pittsburgh every year for their draft day. No girls allowed. Just the guys and their fantasy football dreams. PG told me about his weekend plans and then popped the question: Could he call me during his fantasy football draft to get my opinion on his picks? I was floored! The guy who loved sports and knew more about sports than anyone I had ever met wanted MY opinion on his draft picks! Of course I said yes! It was a real turning point for us.

The real "talk" was a few days after he got back from his fantasy football draft weekend. It was a major milestone. PG told me he had never met anyone like me. I was so helpful to him on draft day and he didn't want that to end. So, PG did what any guy would do in that situation. He gave me his screen name and password to this fantasy football account so I could keep an eye on his team and offer my thoughts whenever I wanted to. If that's not love, I don't know what is. Seriously?!

But back to the worldwide leader. Of course you've heard of ESPN. The all sports, all the time, channel has revolutionized the life of the fan. ESPN dubbed themselves "The Worldwide Leader In Sports." Many sports fans, me included, occasionally refer to ESPN as "the worldwide leader." The reference breaks things up a bit and shows, with a bit of wit, that you aren't merely a casual fan.

While it is, indeed, true that ESPN offers 24 hours of sports coverage, it is imperative to note that some of those hours, in my opinion, suck. Plain and simple. At the risk of offending tens of people, I don't care to watch billiards, bowling, fishing, hunting, poker (even though it can suck me in sometimes and won't let me turn it off!), curling or the world's strongest man competitions. The percentage of people that actually care about these events is quite small. The need to fill air time can cause them to take desperate measures. This typically happens in the summer months when the only notable sports being played are baseball, golf and NASCAR.

There are some shows that the worldwide leader does tremendously well. No doubt you are aware of the biggie: **SportsCenter**. The hour long broadcast covers sports highlights using different anchors. The anchors commentate on a myriad of replays with straight sports talk mixed with comical banter. It's not uncommon to hear phrases such as:

"Cooler than the other side of the pillow."

"Dunk you very much." – basketball

"Bartender! Put it on ice!" – hockey

"Bartender! Make mine a double!" – baseball

Typically, the 11PM show is repeated several times until 10AM the following morning (weekdays). Occasionally ESPN throws the viewer a curve ball by replaying some sporting event in the wee hours of the morning. When my insomnia kicks in, I notice these things.

I first became aware of the replay trend during the Christmas holidays several years ago. My family had all gathered with cousins, aunts, uncles and grandparents from my mom's side of the family. The grownups were in the kitchen preparing the infamous Christmas Eve breakfast. (I kid you not. It's one of the best meals of the entire year.) The kids, who ranged from newborn to 30-something, were in the family room watching, you guessed it, ESPN. My cousin Jonathan proceeded to predict, with amazing accuracy, which highlights would be shown and what silly comments certain star athletes would make. Rather than pretending to be Miss Cleo, Jonathan informed us that his newborn daughter had kept him up most of the night and that this was the sixth time he had seen the same episode of SportsCenter. I thought that was cool.

Because SportsCenter is the most popular show on ESPN and comprehensively covers everything I may or may not have noticed in the world of sports, I watch it while I put on my makeup in the morning. No, it doesn't take me an hour to put on my face. But, I keep the TV on for as long as I can. This personal habit has been a great conversation piece on dates or at parties. While on my first date with Beach Guy, I casually mentioned that I heard something on SportsCenter that morning. He looked at me questioningly. I laughed and said, "I know! I know! It's so silly but I watch SportsCenter when I put on my makeup in the mornings!" And then I promptly moved on to discuss what I had heard on the show. (It's very crucial to not harp on that tidbit. Just toss it in casually and be done with it.)

A couple of weeks later, when BG was professing his undying love for me, he admitted that this was one of the things that he thought was so cool. Okay, okay…well, not so much professing his undying love, but he certainly came clean about liking this little thing about me!

While this makes great conversation, a serious word of caution must be given. If you are going to tell a guy that you heard something on SportsCenter or on any ESPN program, you have to know a bit more about the topic than the phrase you caught in a minute or two. Several girlfriends of mine have watched SportsCenter for two or three minutes before heading out on a date or to a party so that they will have "easy" things to talk about with guys. Sometimes this goes off without a hitch. But, there have been occasions where the target guy got excited or miffed about the chosen topic and wanted to know more about what SportsCenter said or, worse, more about the unsuspecting girl's opinion on the matter.

SportsCenter also covers sports and human interest segments that the average sports fan may not care about. My friend Stephanie watched a few minutes of SportsCenter before going to a party where she would be seeing her crush, Dog Guy. After great conversation with him, Stephanie was ready to pull out all the stops. She proceeded to tell him that she was so impressed with some IndyCar driver's interview and that some team was arguably the best team in the WNBA. DG was speechless. And not in a good way. Stephanie's sports choices were way off base. It's the rare person that cares about an IndyCar race or the WNBA standings. And I don't know any of them. Luckily, she came to her senses and laughed it off. She and DG had an intense four month relationship. The break up had nothing to do with sports.

Taking the initiative to start a conversation about sports is, without a doubt, impressive to most guys. Just be prepared so that you can carry your end of the conversation without looking silly. It's a safe bet that you will score major points with the male population by knowing details about the four major sports: football, basketball, baseball and hockey. Well, at least three of those four sports, anyway. Hockey is a different breed. Sports like golf and NASCAR are also impressive conversation pieces. Soccer and tennis are great to play but are not really talked about in the US. It helps to know your audience.

The worldwide leader offers other programs apart from SportsCenter. **Pardon the Interruption (PTI)** and **Around the Horn** are 30 minute programs shown on weekdays that approach the major sports stories of the day with people arguing the various points of each topic. The arguing is highly entertaining, in my opinion, and often infused with pieces of pop culture and strong humor. I admit I had to get used to these programs. But now, I love them and watch them every chance I get.

Jim Rome is the host of his own television show called Jim Rome Is Burning (JRIB). It appears on ESPN on weekdays. But I bring up Rome for his radio program, not for his television show. Romie or Van Smack, as he is so affectionately referred to, has a three hour radio show (The Jim Rome Show) on weekdays that covers sports. The show is both informative and hilarious. I am an admitted "Clone" (a loyal listener of the program) and find myself laughing out loud every single time I am in "the jungle" (code for listening to the show). The casual sports fan may or may not be aware of Jim Rome. The vast majority of avid fans will know of and have an opinion about Romie and his radio program. I happen to like him.

Mike and Mike in the Morning is a radio program on ESPN radio that has made the transition into being simulcast on ESPN2 weekdays from 6AM-10AM. Hosted by Mike Greenberg (Greeny) and Mike Golic (Golic), the show covers all of the relevant stories of the sports world, while incorporating bits of pop culture and friendly banter. They also make sure that important highlights are replayed for the television audience a few times every hour. Greeny and Golic make me laugh out loud while informing me about new events and statistics. Until they snagged a slot on ESPN2, my morning makeup routine was choreographed solely with SportsCenter. Now I am able to watch Mike and Mike while I, during said routine, am endlessly entertained as they argue with each other about everything under the sun. I also enjoy the side bets they place with each other about any given sporting event. I strongly encourage you to give it a shot.

College Game Day is a two hour program that comes on at 10 AM Eastern every Saturday of football season. Hosted by Chris Fowler (Chris), Kirk Herbstreit (Kirk or the quarterback) and Lee Corso

(Coach), the show discusses all of the games that will be played that day. At the end of the show, Kirk and Coach go through each game and predict who they think will win. The appeal of the show is two-fold:

1) College Game Day goes on location. Every week they are at a different university for a big game. There are thousands of cheering fans that crowd around the outdoor set. This makes for a high energy show.

2) Kirk Herbstreit is arguably the most attractive and most informative broadcaster in college football. I have a few girlfriends who watch the program for the eye candy alone. Kirk, a former quarterback at Ohio State, is also very clear and concise with his football analysis. He makes things easy for fans to understand and always relays valuable information to the viewers.

In my opinion…

Neil Everett is my favorite SportsCenter anchor. He makes me laugh. I have a movie star crush on him.

Woody Page on Around the Horn is funny. I was glad he was the first to get 200 wins on the show.

It was sad to see Dan Patrick leave ESPN in July 2007.

I like when SportsCenter informs me that such and such game will be played at 7PM Eastern, 1PM Hawaiian.

College Game Day is my favorite show and I set my alarm clock to make sure I am awake to watch it every week during football season.

I like calling ESPN "the worldwide leader" sometimes, but not all the time.

THE SPORT: FOOTBALL

It's safe to say that the typical guy in America is interested in or keeps up with college football or the NFL. Most guys do a heck of a lot more than that. They are fans. They follow certain teams. They wear the gear. They play fantasy football. They are passionate, enthusiastic, and over the top.

Football season never comes soon enough. Football is the glorious rainfall that ends the drought of a summer of regular season baseball, NASCAR and golf. The months leading up to football are like the days before Christmas for a kid. The excitement and anticipation build to extreme levels. All you have to do is check out my Facebook status in the days leading up to the season to witness my excitement. It is palpable. I am ready to crawl out of my skin.

Fall and early winter weekends are dominated by football. There is a Thursday night game for college, Saturday games for college, Sunday games for the NFL and a Monday night game for the NFL. If you can learn to tolerate or, better yet, become interested in football, it makes those several months much more bearable.

The NFL preseason begins in early August and is immediately followed by the regular season. The playoffs follow the regular season and the Super Bowl has been pushed back to early February. College football begins in early September. There are no preseason games. The post season doesn't include playoffs. It is comprised of a myriad of bowl games, which includes the BCS (Bowl Championship Series) games that are supposed to determine the uncontested national champion. Instead, it usually spawns endless debate about the true champion.

Division 1 or D1 college football is the only sport without playoffs. I happen to be of the opinion that a small playoff series to determine a national champion would be great for the sport. But, the payout to play in a bowl game is hundreds of thousands of dollars. It seems like there is more money in the bowl system. Which means we'll never get a playoff. I think that thirty of the bowl games can continue as normal. The difference would be to hold a playoff for the top eight teams at the end of the season. I've heard rumblings that the University presidents oppose the playoff idea because they don't want their student-athletes to miss class. They aren't in class for several weeks in December or January. The BCS games are close to mid-January as it is. And Division I AA has an extremely successful playoff system. Reason would seem to indicate that we could take some ideas from them.

There is no college football preseason like in the NFL. But college football has preseason rankings that seem a bit unfair. A list ranking the top 25 teams in college football is published several weeks before the season begins. I understand that the list is based on the previous year results. It also takes into consideration any new players a team recruited and players that are no longer there. But, a team that doesn't begin the season in the top 25 (really, the top 12 or 15) can all but kiss any chance of a BCS bowl game goodbye. Shouldn't we wait to rank teams after they have played a couple of games? It seems this would make more sense and give everyone a fighting chance.

As far as the NFL preseason goes, the four games they play are more like four dress rehearsals. The teams play in full pads and uniforms. They play other NFL teams. They charge full price for tickets. But the starters and stars see minimal playing time, if any at all. So fans are forced to pay top dollar to watch a game where the main goal, the only goal, is not to get hurt. It's not about winning. At all. The preseason is about avoiding injury. So why is there a four week preseason if no one takes it seriously? And why make fans pay regular season prices when they are not watching regular season games? The almighty dollar rears its ugly head again.

When you become interested in football, you can get by without having to discuss the sport year round. And even when the sport is in season, it's not like there are tons of games to watch. Each team only plays once a week unless it's their bye week, and then they don't play at all. After the season is over, it's easy to talk about the pros and the cons of bowl games and all controversies wrought by the BCS for a good month. The same is true for the NFL (minus the BCS part). Conversation revolves around reliving the good from the season and picking apart the bad. During the summer months when football withdrawal gives fans the shakes, you revel in the bits of off season news and make statements like, "Man! Football season can't come fast enough!" or "How do you think the <insert favorite team here> will look this year?"

One of the most loved traditions surrounding football is tailgating. Guys and girls, alike, enjoy this event. What's not to love? Being outside with tons of people in the fall months, grilling out and sipping cold beverages…It's what makes America good. Instead of sleeping in on Saturdays, I have friends who make sure they are out at their predetermined tailgating spot, set up and ready to go by 8 AM no matter what time kickoff is. Bright and early. They are as passionate about the tailgating as they are the game itself. This is an activity that girls tend to enjoy, too, regardless of their interest in the game. Use this to your advantage. Jump into the tailgating festivities, if nothing else. And feel free to do it up right! I know a few girls who put on a show each week. They stray from typical football food fare and put out a spread that would make the Rachel Ray proud. So take some ownership and put your own spin on things. You'll learn to love it a whole lot more!

Tailgating is fun. But talking to guys about sports is another adventure. I went on a few dates with one I'll call Fancy Guy one summer. He always took me to really fancy places on dates. I was wined and dined. He was a gentleman and old fashioned, believing that a woman deserved to be given nice things and taken to nice places. Ummm… Okay! One evening we were at yet another fancy dinner and FG asked me what my dream date was. Well, football season had just started, so I answered him the only way I knew how. Football, wings and beer. To say he was shocked is an understatement. It was a combination of good shock and bad shock. He had put all of this effort into taking me on extravagant dates when what I really wanted was football, wings and beer. But, the boy loved his football, so he was thrilled to know that I would be interested in doing that.

Okay, okay…I admit that part of the reason I answered that way was for the sheer reaction of it all. What girl doesn't love getting dressed up and taken out on the town? So maybe my dream date isn't really football, wings and beer. But it was appropriate at the time. And his reaction was priceless!

Don't get me wrong. I'm not a tomboy. I love getting dressed up and going to nice places. But I like it all in moderation. It's all about balance. It's about the sidelines and the stilettos. Had FG only taken me to dives, hole in the walls and sports bars, my answer to the dream date question would have been something about getting dressed up and going somewhere fancy. It just so happened that the opposite was true. And our very next date? Well, it was just what I wanted: football, wings and beer.

In 2005, the Pittsburgh Steelers won the Super Bowl. It was Super Bowl XL. (Super Bowls are always written in Roman numerals.) They played and won the game on February 5, 2006 in Detroit. (Yes, I know it's weird that the 2005 Steelers won the Super Bowl that was played in the calendar year 2006. It's just how it is.) For the entire 2005 football season, I went to the same sports bar every week after church to watch the Steelers. It got to the point that the waitress knew my name and the names of my friends. Her name was Molly and she would save us tables in her section every week. The place got really crowded so I was grateful that I didn't have to arrive way early to save seats! Showing up regularly at a place that shows all of the games was a great way to meet people (errr…guys). Not too bad at all.

I happen to be very superstitious about sports. I wear certain things if they seem to be good luck. I make my friends change seats if my team isn't doing well. It's a little over the top, but in a game I have no control over, it makes me feel like I have a teeny bit of power. That year, I wore a particular pair of really great jeans with some vintage cowboy boots and a Steelers jersey (kid's size so it was more girlie and fitted) for every game. (Maybe that's how Molly learned my name so quickly. It's not like I made it hard by changing clothes each week.) I don't even think my jewelry changed. And yes, I wore jewelry. I made sure to look cute and girlie with hair, makeup and jewelry since I was wearing a football jersey. Of course, I washed my outfit every week because not doing so is just gross. But, everyone knew I wore the same thing week in and week out as my little way of spurring on the team.

I remember Super Bowl XL Sunday like it was yesterday. My mom called me after church to see how I was feeling. It was game day after all. You would have thought I was actually playing in the game based on how nervous I felt. I couldn't eat. I felt like I was going to throw up (Kind of like how I feel on a first date). I was pacing around the house. Couldn't sit still. Seriously. I was that nervous. The first thing my mom asked me was if I was already suited up in my game day uniform. I was. Tradition. Superstition. Call it what you will. It was the year that my outfit helped the Steelers win the Super Bowl.

The People:

Players – Each team has eleven players on the field for offense and defense. However, the combinations of positions on the field at any given point varies greatly.

Offense – Their goal is to score points.

- **Center (C)** – He's the guy that snaps (or "hikes") the ball between his legs to the quarterback. Then he blocks defensive players.

- **Offensive Guards (OG) and Offensive Tackles (OT)** – There are two of these guys. They line up on each side of the Center (tackles line up beside the guards). They block the other team and keep the defense from getting to the Quarterback. They also block so that their team can have somewhere to run the ball, if that's what the play calls for.

- **Offensive Line (OL, "O Line")** – The line is made up of the center, guards and tackles whose primary focus is to protect the quarterback and allow plays (throwing or passing) to happen. If the O Line doesn't do their job, the quarterback may get hurried (rushed into making a play before he's ready) or sacked (tackled by the defense). Without the O Line doing their jobs, there wouldn't be anywhere to run with the ball on rushing plays.

- **Tight Ends (TE)** – They line up by the tackles but can also catch the ball. Their jobs vary depending upon the play. They may block, tackle, and run to catch the ball or catch the ball then run with it.

- **Wide Receivers (WR)** – Their main job is to get open so they can catch the ball when the quarterback throws it to them. The pass from the quarterback may be long or short. Once they catch the ball, they run with it and are often, with the running backs, the fastest guys on the field.

- **Full Back (FB)** – This guy does a few different things. When he is in action, his job is to block, to make room for the running back, to run with the ball or to catch short passes.

- **Running Back (RB)** – Their main job is to take the ball when the quarterback hands it off to them and run with it. These are called rushing plays. Along with wide receivers, running backs are the fastest guys on the field.

- **Quarterback (QB)** – He is the ringleader on the Offense. He manages the game on the field. The QB gets the ball off the snap from the center and then sets up the plays. Rushing plays are when the QB hands the ball off to another player, or keeps it himself, and runs with it. Passing plays are when the QB passes the ball to another player who catches it and tries to keep running with it.

Defense (D) – Their job is to keep the offense from scoring points.

- **Defensive Ends (DE) and Defensive Tackles (DT)** – They make up the Defensive Line and line up across from the Offensive Line. The D Line tries to get to the quarterback to stop plays. They also try to stop any running plays from coming up the middle of the field since that is where they line up.

- **Linebackers (LB)** – These are great defenders who do different things. Their roles include trying to get to the quarterback, covering wide receivers and stopping run plays. They are lined up horizontally facing the Offense (behind the D-line) and can be referred to by their place in that line – outside or middle.

- **Cornerbacks (CB)** – They are used to mainly run with wide receivers and prevent them from catching passes. They will help stop run plays when no passing is taking place.

- **Safety (S)** – Safeties line up farthest from the D Line. Strong Safeties are bigger and help stop big runs. Free Safeties are quicker and help stop long passes.

Special Teams – They make the plays that aren't specifically related to Offense or Defense.

- **Kicking Team** – These guys are on the field for kickoffs. A kickoff occurs at the beginning of the game, at the beginning of the second half, and after a team scores. The team that scores kicks the ball to the other team so they have a chance to score, too. One team simply kicks the ball to the other team.

- **Punting Team** – These guys are on the field to punt the ball to the other team on 4th down. The ball is punted on 4th down because the Offense wasn't able to go ten yards with the ball and get a first down.

- **Receiving Team** – These are the guys on the field to catch the ball and run with it after kickoffs and punts.

- **Field Goal Unit** – These are the guy on the field whenever the Offense is attempting to make a field goal to score three points.

- **Kicker** – He places the ball on the tee and runs up to the ball to kick it really far. A kicker comes in for the kickoff at the beginning of the game, at the beginning of the second half and after every time his team scores. He also kicks the ball through the uprights for each attempt of a point after touchdown. He also attempts field goals.

- **Punter** – He holds the ball in his hands and punts it on fourth down. This is a different type of kick. Different skills are used, so it is a separate position and a different person from the other kicker.

The Words:

500 – a term used to indicate that a team has an equal number of wins and losses. This phrase was derived from looking at a statistics sheet where win-loss percentage was indicated as .500 meaning 50%. The goal for any team is to always be "above 500" for the season, which means that the team has more wins than losses. A team that is "under 500" is having a very bad year. Even just being 500 on the season is very mediocre.

AP Poll – a ranking system determined by sports writers across the nation. The sportswriters vote on the top 25 teams. Exclusive to NCAA football.

BCS Bowl Game – Four bowl games that make up the most prestigious bowl games each year. On a rotating schedule, one BCS bowl game is selected to be the title game for the national championship each year. The four BCS bowl games are: The Rose Bowl held in California,

The Fiesta Bowl in Arizona, The Orange Bowl in Florida, and The Sugar Bowl in Louisiana. Only teams from a BCS Conference can play in BCS bowl games. One of my personal goals is to attend all four BCS bowl games. So far I have not attended any of them. Dreaming big. Exclusive to NCAA football.

BCS Conference – one of the six major conferences in NCAA Division 1 football. Those conferences are ACC, Big East, Big Ten, Big 12, PAC 10, and SEC. Unlike the other conferences that play their regular season with the hope of getting into a general bowl game, the schools of the BCS conferences play for an automatic spot in one of the four BCS bowl games. Schools in BCS conferences are also eligible to play in the general bowl games. Typically, there is a team from a non-BCS conference with a perfect or near perfect record at the end of the regular season that gets the shaft because of how the system works. It makes for great conversation. Exclusive to NCAA football.

BCS Title Game – one of the BCS bowl games that is selected as the national championship game. The specific game rotates between the four BCS bowl games each year. Exclusive to NCAA football.

Blitz – when guys from the defense run straight for the quarterback, trying to sack him or make him mess up.

Bowl Game – a single game played by two teams from different conferences after the regular season ends. Bowl games are a goal for every college team because they get to travel, play a team outside of their conference and receive a very large monetary payout. There were 32 bowl games played in the 2006 season. Exclusive to NCAA football.

Bye – the week that a team doesn't have to play during the regular season. The NFL regular season is seventeen weeks, but each team only plays sixteen games. Most NCAA teams play the maximum allowed twelve games.

Coaches Poll – a ranking system for the top 25 teams determined by the Board of Coaches. The Board of Coaches is comprised of head coaches from D1 schools. Duke, a team notorious for their losing records in football, receives one vote from Steve Spurrier every season despite the fact that they are among the worst football teams. Spurrier coached at Duke in the 80's and has a soft spot in his heart for the Blue Devils. Exclusive to NCAA football.

Completion – when the ball is thrown and caught by guys on the same team.

D1 – this term refers to Division 1 in college sports. Division 1 schools are at the top of the tier in terms of power, money, facilities and success. D1 schools receive the most television time and media coverage.

Dead Ball – the time during the game when a play has ended and no other play has started yet.

Delay of Game – a penalty on the offense when they don't start a play before the play clock runs out.

Down – one play – the Offense has 4 downs (4 tries, 4 plays) to make the football move forward 10 yards. If the Offense can't move the ball 10 yards, it goes to the other team. That's bad. Every time they move it past the specified 10 yards (past the orange sticks on the sidelines or yellow line on TV) they are awarded a "first down." This means they get to keep going. The goal, of course, is to keep moving the ball down the field to score a touchdown. And, if not a touchdown, then a field goal.

Downing the Ball – a strategic play used at the end of the half or the end of the game when the team on Offense is trying to score before the clock runs out and needs to quickly stop the clock so that the time doesn't run out. It takes time to move all eleven players down the field, so it is important not to waste valuable seconds off the clock. To stop the clock and get everyone in place for a set play, the quarterback will take the snap and intentionally throw the ball directly on the ground.

End Zone – the ten yards on both ends of the football field that the Offense tries to reach with the football and the Defense tries to protect.

Extra Point – the one point awarded to the Offense for kicking the ball through the uprights after a touchdown. It is also known as a P.A.T. (Point After Touchdown)

Face Mask – a penalty when a player grabs another player's face mask in order to drag him down and tackle him. Depending on the severity of the face mask attack, the penalty can be 5 yards or 15 yards.

Fair Catch – a signal made (usually waving his arms in the air in some way) by a receiver who is catching a ball that has been punted down field. After signaling for a fair catch, defenders running downfield are not allowed to hit the receiver. The receiver is not allowed to run with the ball once he catches it after calling a fair catch.

False Start – a penalty given to a player on the offense if he moves from the line or a set position before the play begins. An offensive player may try to move a little bit to make the Defense think the play has begun and to draw the Defense offsides. The penalty is 5 yards in the wrong direction.

Field Goal – a kick between the uprights that is awarded three points.

Franchise – a professional team.

Franchise Player – a superstar on a team. This term also refers to a label a player may receive in contract negations. I won't bore you with all of that. Exclusive to professional sports.

Front Office – the administrative and business side of a sports franchise. Exclusive to professional sports.

Fumble – what happens when the player with the ball (usually the quarterback, running back or wide receiver since they are the guys who touch the ball the most) in his hands drops it during a play. Once the ball hits the ground, everyone goes for it. Whoever gets the ball from the ground is said to have recovered the fumble.

Hail Mary Pass – a really, really long high pass way down the field made by the quarterback while he prays that someone on his team will catch it.

Home Team – the home team is always listed second or on the bottom.

Hurry-Up Offense – a series of plays by the Offense where they don't get together in a huddle between the ending of one play and the beginning of the next. A hurry-up Offense is usually done when there are two minutes or less left on the clock. The Offense does all of these plays quickly so that they can try to score points before the clock runs out.

Icing the Kicker – calling a timeout right before the other team is about to kick a major (game winning or game tying) field goal. This is a mental tactic that forces the kicker to think about the monumental task at hand. The opposing team is hoping to get under the kicker's skin and break down his mental game.

Idle – the week that a team doesn't have to play during the regular season; also known as the bye week.

In Bounds Rule – a college player must catch a ball with at least one foot inbounds for the play to be a completion, while an NFL player must catch the ball with both feet in bounds.

Incomplete Pass – a term used interchangeably with the word "incomplete" to signify that the ball that was thrown was not caught.

Intentional Grounding – a penalty when the quarterback "throws the football away" in an area where no one can catch it (the sidelines or the ground) because none of his receivers are open and he can't run anywhere with the ball.

Interception – when a player from the wrong team catches the ball thrown by the quarterback. An interception is often referred to as "a pick."

Line of Scrimmage – the imaginary line on the field where the football is placed and around which the Offense and Defense line up. Neither side is allowed to cross the line of scrimmage before the play begins. The quarterback is not allowed to throw the ball if he crosses the line of scrimmage.

Offsides – a penalty given to a player on the Defense for moving across the line of scrimmage before the play has begun. The penalty is five yards in the wrong direction.

Option – a play where the quarterback has the ball and has the choice to pass it, hand it off or run with it.

Overtime – the period of play after the regular game (often called regulation) used to break a tie. College teams each get one possession with the ball. After two overtimes, college teams must attempt a two point conversion after a touchdown, instead of an extra point. The NFL overtime is a fifteen minute period where the first team to score wins. This is called "sudden death." A coin flip determines who has possession of the ball first.

Pass Interference – the act of coming into contact (including pushing and tripping) with the player trying to catch the ball so that he won't be able to catch it. While it happens most often with a defensive player trying to stop an offensive player from catching a ball, there are a fair amount of plays that involve the offensive player trying to keep an interception from happening, so they interfere with the defensive player who is in position to make the pick.

Penalty – doing something illegal and receiving a loss of yards.

Play Action – a play where the quarterback gets the ball from the snap and pretends to hand the ball off to another player (the running back) all the while really keeping it for himself. This play tricks the Defense and gives the quarterback time to throw the ball.

Playoffs – the tournament in the NFC and AFC to determine who will play in the Super Bowl. The AFC and NFC are each broken down into four divisions (North, South, East and West) of four teams. The winner of each division, determined during the regular season, automatically makes it into the playoffs. There are also two wild card spots in both the NFC and AFC so that a total of six teams from each conference make it to the playoffs. There are three weeks of playoffs before the big Super Bowl game. Exclusive to the NFL.

Preseason – the four weeks of games before the NFL regular season when players get used to all the pads and gear and try not to get hurt. The preseason games are much like a glorified practice. The starters and superstars may play for only the first few minutes of the game so that they don't risk getting hurt. Some stars choose not to play at all. LaDanian Tomlinson of the San Diego Chargers is one of them. When you are as good as LT, the coaching staff and front office will let you get away with choosing not to play in the preseason. The main goal of all preseason games is to not get hurt. Winning doesn't matter. Staying injury free is really the only thing that matters. Exclusive to the NFL.

P.A.T. – the one point awarded to the Offense for kicking the ball through the uprights after a touchdown. It is also known as an extra point.

Pocket – the area around the quarterback when he has the ball in his hands and is looking to pass. The offensive line is supposed to protect the quarterback so he doesn't get hit by the Defense while in the pocket.

Quarterback Sack – when the quarterback is tackled before passing or handing off the football. A sack usually results in a loss of yards, making the Offense have to back up.

Quarterback Rating – a number given to quarterbacks figured from a complicated statistical formula involving his complete passes, incomplete passes, pass attempts, touchdown passes and interceptions. The maximum rating in the NFL is 158.3, while the NCAA doesn't have a maximum.

Quarterback Sneak – a play when the quarterback lines up right under the center's back side, gets the ball at the snap and lunges, jumps, or hurries straight forward behind the center. This play is designed to gain a small amount of yardage.

Red Flag – the flag thrown by the head coach on the sideline signifying that he wants to challenge the official's ruling on the field.

Red Shirt – a term used when a college player sits out a year. He is on the team but is not allowed to play in games. A red shirt year does not count against the player's four years of eligibility. Often times, a coach will red shirt a freshman athlete so that he can develop and grow more and still have four more years of eligibility after that first year. A player seriously injured before the season, or in the first few minutes of the very first game, will be given a medical red shirt so that they can heal and recover for a year and play the next year. A player that transfers from one D1 school to another D1 school must red shirt the first transfer year. (Unless the athlete transfers to another school in the same conference, in which case he would have to red shirt two years.)

Rookie – a professional athlete in his first season.

Safety – the two points awarded to the Defense when the Offense is tackled or fumbles the ball in their own end zone.

Scramble – when the quarterback runs around in the pocket to avoid defenders that the offensive line has let slip by. The quarterback scrambles so that he can find someone open to pass the ball to. If no one is open, he may decide to run with the ball to try to gain a few yards on the play.

Shaken Up – a term typically used when a player is slow to get up indicating that he is not quite normal after a hit or a play but not to the severity of being "hurt" or "injured." This term will be used to describe a multitude of scenarios including, but not limited to, being slow to get up off the field, limping after a play, or favoring an arm or shoulder.

Snap – the passing of the ball between the center's legs (the big guy bent over in the middle of the offense on the line of scrimmage) to the quarterback to start a play. The term is used interchangeably with the term "hike."

Shotgun Formation – the way a quarterback lines up a few yards behind the center to have the ball hiked to him. More common, though, is the quarterback lining up right underneath the center's backside.

Super Bowl – the championship game played between the best team in the AFC and the best team in the NFC.

Tearing Down the Goalposts – a celebratory gesture after a particularly big win where students and fans rush onto the field in mass quantities to rip down the uprights in the end zones. Schools make every attempt to prevent this from happening due to the number of injuries and deaths it can cause. It is also true that each goalpost cost tens of thousands of dollars. Many schools have installed retractable goalposts that can be lowered to the ground at the end of the game, thereby preventing fans from tearing them down.

Three and Out – when a team is on Offense for three downs and then forced to punt because they can't get to the ten yard marker they need to get a first down.

Trick Plays – plays that are infamous, brand new or involve movements that break the traditional patterns. Trick plays are designed to trick the Defense but are very risky. Trick plays include, but are not limited to, the following: Hook and Ladder, Fake Punt, Fake Field Goal, Wide Receiver Pass, and Flea Flicker. Boise State used two trick plays at the end of the game to beat Oklahoma in the 2007 Fiesta Bowl.

Two-Point Conversion – the play after a touchdown where the Offense tries to get the football into the end zone again, instead of kicking it through the uprights. Successfully done, this is awarded 2 points instead of 1 point for the P.A.T. If your team is down by 2 or 5 or 9 with half of the 4th quarter to go (or less) it is appropriate to yell, "Go for 2!" If they go for 2 and get it, they will have tied the game or put themselves in a position to get the ball back and kick a field goal to tie (if they were down by 5) or put themselves in a position to get the ball back and score a touchdown plus extra point to tie (if they were down by 9).

Uprights – the tall goal posts at either end of the football field. A kicker will try to kick it through the uprights to gain three points on a field goal or one point for the point after touchdown (also known as extra point and P.A.T.).

Vince Lombardi Trophy – the trophy given to the winner of the Super Bowl each year. The trophy is named to memorialize and honor Vince Lombardi (thank you, Captain Obvious), the legend who coached the Green Bay Packers. And ladies, the creator of said trophy is none other than Tiffany & Co. Nice!

Visiting Team – the visiting team is always listed first or on the top.

West Coast Offense – an Offense that is designed around shorter passes and longer runs once the ball is caught, as opposed to throwing the ball a long way down the field. It was made famous by Bill Walsh, a former coach for the San Francisco 49ers.

Wildcard – the two NFL playoff spots awarded to the teams in each conference with the best records that did not win the division.

Yellow Flag – the flag thrown on the field by the officials signifying that a penalty has taken place.

The Signals:

The images below offer just a few of the signals the officials on the field may use. These are some of the most frequently used. There are tons more, but no one needs to know them.

DELAY OF GAME

FALSE START

FIRST DOWN

HOLDING

INTENTIONAL GROUNDING

OFFSIDE

PASS INTERFERENCE

PERSONAL FOUL

ROUGHING THE KICKER

SAFETY

TOUCHDOWN

UNSPORTSMANLIKE CONDUCT

The Outfits:

The stickers on helmets go to players who have made outstanding plays. It's a good thing to have a lot of stickers on a helmet.

The black paint stuff on a player's face (a stripe of black under each eye) allegedly helps keep the glare out of his eyes. I think they do it because it just looks really tough.

The Hard to Miss:

The Oregon Ducks boast colors of bright Kelly green and true yellow. That combination of the football team in tight pants and jerseys is often unsightly. They may qualify for the worst uniform award.

The Clemson Tigers have always had orange as their main color. But, in the past few years, the Tigers have begun to incorporate more of their secondary color, which happens to be purple. It is so very interesting to see tough football players in tight purple pants! I actually like that the purple has made a comeback.

The ECU Pirates use purple and yellow as their colors. Occasionally, on their home field, the Pirates will wear purple from head to toe. While not the worst looking uniforms out there, it certainly leaves an impression!

The Pros: NFL Conferences and Divisions

AFC North:
Baltimore Ravens
Cincinnati Bengals
Cleveland Browns
Pittsburgh Steelers

AFC South:
Houston Texans
Indianapolis Colts
Jacksonville Jaguars
Tennessee Titans

AFC East:
Buffalo Bills
Miami Dolphins
New England Patriots
New York Jets

AFC West:
Denver Broncos
Kansas City Chiefs
Oakland Raiders
San Diego Chargers

NFC North:
Chicago Bears
Green Bay Packers
Detroit Lions
Minnesota Vikings

NFC South:
Atlanta Falcons
Carolina Panthers
New Orleans Saints
Tampa Bay Buccaneers

NFC East:
Dallas Cowboys
New York Giants
Philadelphia Eagles
Washington Redskins

NFC West:
Arizona Cardinals
San Francisco 49ers
Seattle Seahawks
St. Louis Rams

The College Kids:

Atlantic Coast Conference (ACC) – The ACC is made up of 12 D1 schools and has a reputation for being a dominant conference in men's basketball. The dominant rivalry is between Duke and UNC in basketball, followed closely by a heated rivalry between NC State and UNC in anything. Clemson, whose football team occasionally wears bright purple pants, has a big in-state rivalry against the University of South Carolina from the SEC. FSU is led by Bobby Bowden (retired in 2009-2010 season), one of the oldest, most well respected coaches in all of football. In football, Miami, Virginia Tech and Florida State traditionally dominate the conference. Member schools: Boston College (BC) Eagles, Clemson Tigers, Duke Blue Devils, Florida State (FSU) Seminoles, Georgia Tech Yellow Jackets, Maryland (UMD) Terrapins, Miami Hurricanes, NC State (State or NCSU) Wolfpack, University of North Carolina (Carolina or UNC) Tarheels, Virginia (UVA) Cavaliers, Virginia Tech Hokies, Wake Forest (Wake or WFU) Demon Deacons.

Big East Conference – The Big East is made up of 16 D1 schools and is widely respected in both football and men's basketball. In years past, a false underdog stigma can be attached to Big East teams. However, when West Virginia, Louisville and Rutgers all flirted with a bid into the national championship game for the 2006 football season, the Big East gained tremendous respect as an up and coming, if not flat out powerful, football conference. One popular note of the Big East is that Notre Dame is a member in all sports except football. Notre Dame, along with Villanova and Georgetown, have football programs that are not associated with the Big East. (A weird exception to the rule.) Member schools: Cincinnati Bearcats, Connecticut (UConn) Huskies, DePaul Blue Demons, Georgetown Hoyas, Louisville Cardinals, Marquette Golden Eagles, Notre Dame Fighting Irish, Pittsburgh Panthers, Providence Friars, Rutgers Scarlet Knights, St. John's Red Storm, Seton Hall Pirates, University of South Florida Bulls, Syracuse Orange, Villanova Wildcats, West Virginia Mountaineers.

Big Ten Conference – The Big Ten is made up of, you guessed it, 11 D1 schools and has been around the longest. For part of the year it is known as a strong football conference because of Ohio State and Michigan, who have an intense rivalry and the legacy of Penn State who boasts one of the oldest, most well respected college football coaches in Joe Paterno (lingo: JoePa). Michigan also has a heated out of conference rivalry with Notre Dame. During other parts of the year, the Big Ten is heralded for their longstanding basketball talent as found in Michigan, Michigan State and Indiana. The "Fab 5" gained their fame as freshman at Michigan. Indiana basketball has a tremendous movie based upon one of their basketball seasons from decades past. You may have heard of it. It's called Hoosiers. Member schools: Illinois Fighting Illini, Indiana Hoosiers, Iowa Hawkeyes, Michigan Wolverines, Michigan State Spartans, Minnesota Golden Gophers, Northwestern Wildcats, Ohio State Buckeyes, Penn State Nittany Lions, Purdue Boilermakers, Wisconsin Badgers.

Big 12 Conference – The Big 12's made up of 12 D1 schools that are really good at football. It's just how they grow 'em in that part of the country. While players and schools in Texas, Oklahoma, and Kansas have some success on the basketball court, that area is extremely well known for the caliber of football they produce. Member schools: Baylor Bears, Colorado Buffaloes, Iowa State Cyclones, Kansas Jayhawks, Kansas State Wildcats, Missouri Tigers, Nebraska Cornhuskers, Oklahoma Sooners, Oklahoma State Cowboys, Texas Longhorns, Texas A&M Aggies, Texas Tech Red Raiders.

Conference USA (C-USA) – C-USA is made up of 12 D1 schools that often fly under the radar. These teams are often considered underdogs or "mid-majors" even though they are a part of a D1 conference. Member schools: University of Alabama at Birmingham (UAB) Trailblazers, Central Florida (UCF) Knights, East Carolina (ECU) Pirates, Houston Cougars, Marshall Thundering Herd, Memphis Tigers, Rice Owls, Southern Methodist University (SMU) Mustangs, Southern Mississippi (USM) Golden Eagles, University of Texas at El Paso (UTEP – pronounced you tep) Miners, Tulane Green Wave, Tulsa Golden Hurricane.

Mid-American Conference (MAC – pronounced mack) – The MAC is made up of 12 D1 schools that keep most teams on upset alert. Often thought of as mid-majors or underdogs, these teams often surprise their opponents and pull out a win. Member schools: Akron Zips, Ball State Cardinals, Bowling Green Falcons, Buffalo Bulls, Central Michigan Chippewas, Eastern Michigan Eagles, Kent State Golden Flashes, Miami (of Ohio) University Red Hawks, Northern Illinois Huskies, Ohio University Bobcats, Toledo Rockets, Western Michigan Broncos.

Mountain West Conference – The Mountain West is made up of nine D1 schools that comprise the newest of all of the D1 conferences having begun in 1999. Member schools: Air Force Falcons, Brigham Young (BYU) Cougars, Colorado State Rams, New Mexico Lobos, San Diego State University (SDSU) Aztecs, Texas Christian (TCU) Horned Frogs, University of Nevada Las Vegas (UNLV) Rebels, Utah Utes, Wyoming Cowboys.

Pacific Ten Conference (Pac 10) – The Pac 10 is made up of 10 schools and examined by the rest of the world for their strength in football. Because USC tends to top the football charts at some point year after year, the entire conference is closely scrutinized for strength and football ability. But, this conference also boasts great basketball talent and tradition as well. It is also interesting to note Oregon's colors of green and yellow, as they make for some of the flashiest football uniforms to date. Pay careful attention to Stanford's nickname (Cardinal), as it is never plural. When the national media refers to USC, they are almost always talking about University of Southern California as opposed to the University of South Carolina. Member schools: Arizona Wildcats, Arizona State (ASU) Sun Devils, University of California Berkeley (Cal) Golden Bears, Oregon Ducks, Oregon State Beavers, Stanford Cardinal, University of California Los Angeles (UCLA) Bruins, University of Southern California (USC) Trojans, Washington Huskies, Washington State Cougars.

Southeastern Conference (SEC) – The SEC is notorious for being a football powerhouse and producing dominant teams that are talked about on the national stage year after year. Almost every match up in the conference is an intense rivalry. There are two that come to mind immediately: Auburn-Alabama and Florida-Georgia, the latter football game being known and recognized as "The World's Largest Outdoor Cocktail Party." It is interesting to note that it is not uncommon to find guys and girls dressing up to attend football games in the SEC. Member schools: Alabama Crimson Tide, Arkansas Razorbacks, Auburn Tigers, Florida Gators, Georgia (UGA) Bulldogs, Kentucky Wildcats, Louisiana State University (LSU) Tigers, Mississippi State University Bulldogs, University of South Carolina (USC) Gamecocks, Tennessee Volunteers (Vols), University of Mississippi (Ole Miss) Rebels, Vanderbilt Commodores.

Sun Belt Conference – The Sun Belt Conference is made up of 13 D1 schools that are typically thought of as underdogs or mid-majors. Member schools: University of Arkansas at Little Rock Trojans, Arkansas State Indians, Denver Pioneers, Florida Atlantic University (FAU) Owls, Florida International University (FIU) Golden Panthers, University of Louisiana at Lafayette Rajin' Cajuns, University of Louisiana at Monroe Warhawks, Middle Tennessee State University (MTSU) Blue Raiders, New Orleans Privateers, North Texas Mean Green, University of South Alabama Jaguars, Troy Trojans, Western Kentucky Hilltoppers.

Western Athletic Conference (WAC – pronounced wack) – The WAC is made up of nine D1 schools that are known to be heartbreakers in the football world. They have proven themselves against traditional powerhouse teams. Boise State is a team that everyone knows because they play on a football field that is made of artificial blue turf, or "smurf turf" as it is sometimes called. The blue field receives a lot of media attention. Member schools: Boise State Broncos, California State University Fresno (Fresno State) Bulldogs, Hawaii Rainbows or Rainbow Warriors, Idaho Vandals, Louisiana Tech Bulldogs, Nevada Wolfpack, New Mexico State Aggies, San Jose State University Spartans, Utah State Aggies.

Be aware that many teams share mascots. Tigers are claimed by Clemson, LSU and Auburn, to name a few. Wolfpack is shared by Nevada and NC State.

Be aware that some schools share initials. This is crucial knowledge because it's embarrassing to offer your thoughts about OSU if you're referring to Ohio State but the game on television is Oklahoma State or Oregon State. ASU is shared by Arizona State and Appalachian State. USC is shared by University of Southern California and University of South Carolina.

THE SPORT: BASKETBALL

College basketball is one of my favorite things on earth. I look forward to it every year. The season starts in November and ends in March/April. Conference tournaments begin the infamous "March Madness" and are followed by the NCAA tournament. One Sunday evening in March, after all of the conference tournaments have finished, there's a show called Selection Sunday. During that one hour television show, the 65 teams that are selected to be a part of the NCAA tournament are revealed. Winners of each conference tournament are guaranteed a spot in the tournament despite whether or not they were ranked at the end of the season. Teams in the top 25 rankings typically get good placements in the tournament unless, of course, there are several teams from one conference that are ranked in the top 25. A really dominant conference may get four or five teams into the NCAA tournament, but it's tough to do. The NCAA tournament is a bracket style tournament that ends with the Final Four (the last four teams who have not lost) and the NCAA championship game. Teams that don't make it to the NCAA tournament may be invited to the NIT (National Invitational Tournament). As another bracket style tournament, the NIT produces great games and a chance for postseason play for many teams.

Professional basketball takes shape in the NBA. The season is much longer, as it begins in October and ends at the end of April after each team has played 82 games. The postseason is made up of eight teams from each conference. The three division winners automatically make the playoffs, while the next five highest ranked teams are also awarded spots. Teams play an opponent from the same conference in a best-of-seven series until two teams remain, one from each conference. The final two teams play in a best-of-seven series for the NBA champion title.

Typically, college basketball is more of a team sport, while the NBA is made up of a bunch of individual stars running the show. There are individual stars on college teams, but coaches recruit players and sign players who will fit into a particular system. Since a player cannot play for more than four years (and often fewer years for the best of the best) there is considerable turnover in players. Therefore, a program must be established into which the players can fit. Superstars are always welcome and special, but teamwork is a priority in college basketball. Players are drafted and traded in the NBA, which makes it harder to have a framework within which the players can work. The NBA tends to build teams around star players, which works because players can stay with a team for as long as they want to, or as long as they are successful and injury-free.

When I was in college, a family friend gave me two tickets to a Duke game at their home court (Cameron Indoor Stadium). To set this up, Duke tickets are impossible to buy unless you are willing and able to pay several hundred to several thousand dollars depending on their opponent. Cameron Indoor Stadium is a place of tradition and legacy. In an industry that chases the almighty dollar by filling seats, bringing in crowds and having the biggest and best facilities, Duke has chosen to keep a smaller stadium (seating 9,314) that has been around since 1940 and keep the atmosphere as arguably the toughest place to play in college basketball. Duke students surround the court on the first level. They camp out for days in an area known as Kryzyzewski-ville (named after the head coach – Mike Kryzyzewski) to get tickets to games. The students are organized. They chant and cheer and heckle in unison and so loudly that opponents can't help but be mentally shaken. The upper level of Cameron Indoor Stadium is filled with alumni and donors of Duke who have given excessive amounts of money to the school and, therefore, have the right to buy tickets to basketball games. So getting tickets to the game comes with a hefty price or by knowing someone who is willing to part with their seats for a game.

Back to my story though. I was in college and I had a major crush on a Guitar Guy. He had dark hair and intense eyes. He could play the guitar and sing. Sigh. We met through mutual friends from church and spent some time together in groups. We had just started hanging out some by ourselves and I loved it. We weren't dating, but I hoped that was the next step. So when the coveted tickets to a Duke home game landed in my hands, I chose to take GG. If he was indeed boyfriend material, it seemed only natural that I share this windfall with him.

One perfect winter evening, we arrived at Cameron. The atmosphere was, as it always is, electric. You'd have to have been made of stone to not feel the excitement in the air. It was and is contagious! We watched the teams warm up and the student section, even in the time before the game started, heckled the opposing team with their clever chants.

Soon the game began. A few seconds into the game there was a whistle on a play. When an official blows a whistle it means that play has to stop briefly because something illegal (like a foul or an out of bounds ball or something) has happened. GG leaned over and asked me what happened. I answered him briefly, assuming he didn't see whatever it was that took place. A little bit later there was another whistle. GG asked me again what happened. And, of course, I sweetly answered him. After the third whistle and GG's third inquiry about what happened I asked him if he could see the court okay. It turned out that GG knew absolutely nothing about basketball. Nothing. Nadda. Zilch. The boy had never been to a live basketball game and hadn't even made it through a whole one on TV. And, for the rest of the game he sat there like a bump on a log. He was miserable.

Wait. How had I missed that? It didn't matter that GG didn't know anything about basketball. The knowledge wasn't a big deal because it should have been so easy to get caught in the palpable excitement. The atmosphere, the energy, and the passion of a game in person...it's contagious! I didn't want to talk statistics, facts and figures with the boy, but I did want to share the experience with someone who would at least pretend to have a tiny bit of interest. Sharing an experience trumps knowledge every time. Heck...He could have even cheered for the other team. Just show some sort of emotion. Hello, Bump. How is your log?

During another visit to Cameron in January of 2004, Wake Forest was playing Duke in a much anticipated game. Wake, with the eyes of the sports world on them, had just lost their first game of the year to a nationally ranked Texas team, but had won an extremely intense, triple overtime, instant classic game against Duke's archrival UNC a few weeks before. The Wake vs. Duke game was expected to be a thriller and the excitement in Cameron was palpable. The Duke students, long dubbed the "Cameron Crazies," were just as prepared as the athletes on their beloved team. You see, the students and fans can't physically play the game on the court, but they can certainly help their team gain the mental edge.

On that particular Saturday afternoon, the teams were on the courts warming up as they do off and on for the 90 minutes leading up to tip off. The Wake Forest players were out on the court going through a typical pre-game routine of warm ups and stretching. The Cameron Crazies got quiet. Which is completely unnatural. Everyone, including the players on the court, began to look at the Duke student section. They had somehow gotten their hands on a regulation size flag of the state of Texas and unrolled it so it spread out in all of its full glory. Remember how Wake Forest was coming into the Duke game having just lost their first game of the year to Texas? That's the conniving, cleverness that the Cameron Crazies use to unnerve opponents and to give their beloved Duke basketball team the mental edge.

While Duke isn't my passion anymore, their basketball program sparked my interest in sports. By choosing to cheer for Duke all those years ago in 5th grade, I began to form opinions about and educate myself on sports. I began to think for myself. I became interested in and excited about sports and about sports talk that is so heavily dominated by guys. Because of that, there will always be a soft spot in my heart for Duke basketball.

So my love for college basketball runs deep and true. I will watch games on TV just for the heck of it. Because I have a competitive streak in me, it's fun for me to choose a team and cheer for them – even if I don't have a vested interest in the game or the teams playing. The underdog is never a bad team to cheer for. I love going to games. At every arena, the excitement is contagious. I've spent Valentine's Day with dates at basketball games. And I've been completely happy with the choice of date activity. By making it work for me, by having an interest in basketball, I'm able to be a part of an activity that tons of guys enjoy.

The People:

Players – ten players are on the court at one time, five playing for each team. These five guys play offense and defense. Their sizes, skills and positions vary. The coach can make substitutions and use any combination of players he feels will get the job done.

- **The point guard** is often the smallest, quickest and best ball handler on the court. He runs the show by bringing the ball up court, setting the offense and calling the plays. It is appropriate to call the point guard a "1" as that number is used interchangeably with the position title. The point guard is part of the back court.

- **The shooting guard** can be small like a point guard or bigger like a forward. He is the best shooter on the court. It is not uncommon to hear great shooting guards called "pure shooters." It is appropriate to call the shooting guard a "2" as that number is used interchangeably with the position title. The shooting guard is part of the back court.

- **The small forward** can do it all. He isn't as small as the guards, nor is he as big and powerful as the power forward and center, but his skill set is the greatest and he can be used to fill in at other positions. It is appropriate to call the small forward a "3" as that number is used interchangeably with the position title. The small forward is part of the front court.

- **The power forward** is typically one of the tallest players on the court, but not quite as big as a true center. He can play down low in the paint like a center does but is quicker and can move easier than the center. The power forward can play outside of the paint or be substituted for a center. It is appropriate to call the power forward a "4" as that number is used interchangeably with the position title. The power forward is part of the front court.

• **The center** is the biggest, strongest player on the court. He is often slower than guys smaller than him, which is why he stays down low in the paint. By staying in that area, the center can take and make shots near the basket on offense, and guard the basket and rebound on defense. It is appropriate to call the center a "5" as that number is used interchangeably with the position title. The center is part of the front court.

The Words:

500 – a term used to indicate that a team has an equal number of wins and losses. This phrase was derived from looking at a statistics sheet where win-loss percentage was indicated as .500 meaning 50%. The goal for any team is to always be "above 500" for the season, which means that the team has more wins than losses. A team that is "under 500" is having a very bad year. Even just being 500 on the season is very mediocre.

Air Ball – a shot taken that misses the basket, backboard and rim.

Alley-oop – a play on offense where one player throws a high pass towards the basket and another player catches the pass up in the air and immediately scores with a slam dunk.

AP Poll – a ranking system determined by sports writers across the nation. The sportswriters vote on the top 25 teams. Exclusive to NCAA basketball.

Assist – the action of passing the ball to the player who scores. It is not unusual for the point guard to be the leader on the team in assists since he often calls and sets up plays.

Backcourt Violation – when an offensive player, with possession of the ball, crosses back over the center court line towards the opponent's basket.

Bench – refers to the players that don't start the game. A bench can be deep or strong, with several players who can successfully substitute for the starters. Or, a bench can be weak if they only have a couple of players they feel comfortable subbing in for the starters.

Block – the action of a defensive player stopping a basket being made by an offensive player. A foul is called when the defensive player makes contact with the offensive player instead of just the ball. If fans believe no contact was made with the offensive player, they will claim the defensive player got "all ball" and that it was a "clean block." A block is also called when a defensive player comes in the way of an offensive player who is moving towards that basket and falls down.

Boxing Out – a maneuver by which one player will put himself between another player and the basket in order to grab the rebound. It is appropriate to yell "box out" to your team as the other team shoots their second free throw.

Buzzer Beater – the term used when the last attempted shot is taken and made just before the game clock signals the end of the game. Christian Laettner's dramatic buzzer beater against Kentucky in 1992 paved the way for Duke to go on to win the National Championship. Like it or not, that buzzer beater has been known as "the shot heard round the world" and is seen repeatedly in promos for NCAA basketball year after year. I still remember where I was, how I was sitting, who I was with and what I was wearing when I watched that. The game, the shot, was that big.

Charge – a foul when an offensive player runs into a defensive player who is standing there ready to defend.

Cinderella – This term refers to an underdog team, a low seeded team, beating their highly ranked opponent in the NCAA men's basketball tournament. If the lower ranked team wins a few games in a row, the media will devote massive amounts of coverage to the team and adopt them as the Cinderella Story.

Coaches' Poll – a ranking system for the top 25 teams determined by the Board of Coaches. The Board of Coaches is comprised of head coaches from D1 schools. Exclusive to NCAA basketball.

D1 – This term refers to Division 1 in college sports. Division 1 schools are at the top of the tier in terms of power, money, facilities and success. D1 schools receive the most television time and media coverage.

Double-Double – when a player records double digit statistics in two different categories.

Double Team – when two defensive players cover one offensive player. A double team (or even a triple team in extreme cases) is used to prevent a highly talented player from making shots and plays. Kobe Bryant is usually double teamed and sometimes triple teamed. I guess if you've been known to score 50 points a game, it's wise if the defense does whatever they can to keep you from scoring.

Field Goal – a basket scored that is worth two or three points. All baskets that are not free throws are called field goals. Field goal percentage is a statistic often used when discussing a player's talent or ability. High field goal percentage means a high number of the shots taken are made. Low field goal percentage means a low number of the shots taken are made.

Final Four – the last weekend of the college basketball season when the last four teams remaining in the NCAA Tournament play to become the national champion. Exclusive to NCAA basketball.

Flagrant Foul – a foul that involves excessive force. Flagrant fouls count towards a player's and team's personal fouls. The penalty for a flagrant foul is awarding the other team the free throws as well as possession of the ball. Once a player receives two flagrant fouls he is ejected from the game. In particularly extreme circumstances, one flagrant foul can lead to immediate ejection from the game.

Foul – unnecessary or illegal contact between two players during the course of a play. The penalty for a foul is either possession of the ball or free throws, depending upon the situation. After a team has six fouls, they go into the bonus. The bonus is for fouls 7-9 and awards the other team the chance to shoot a one and one. A one and one means that a player from the other team will only have the chance to shoot the second free throw if the first one goes in. Once a team has ten fouls they are in the double bonus. The double bonus means that the other team gets two free throws anytime a foul is committed after that. In NCAA basketball, a player is allowed to play with four personal fouls. After receiving the fifth foul, they are ejected from the game. In the NBA, a player is allowed to play with five fouls and is ejected after receiving his sixth foul.

Franchise – a professional team.

Front Office – the administrative and business side of a sports franchise. Exclusive to professional sports.

Home Team – the home team is always listed second or on the bottom.

Icing – calling a timeout just before a player on the other team shoots major free throws at the end of the game. The free throws will have the potential to make the point gap very surmountable, tie the game or take the lead. This is a mental tactic that forces the shooter to think about the monumental task at hand. The opposing team is hoping to get under the shooter's skin and break down his mental game.

Intentional Foul – a deliberate foul on an opposing player. The penalty for an intentional is free throws and possession of the ball.

Jump Ball – at the start of a game it is a method of determining who will gain possession of the ball by tossing the ball in the air and letting two opposing players jump to get it.

Lane – the part of the basketball court that is between the free throw line and the basket. It is often painted a different color and is often called "the paint." Usually the big, tall strong guys, called centers, hang out in the paint to guard the basket or to try to score.

Man-to-Man – a term for a defensive strategy that matches one player on the defense to one player on the offense so that all of the plays by the offense are covered by one man on defense.

March Madness – the time period after the regular basketball season ends when conference tournaments take place and lead into several weeks of NCAA Tournament play. Exclusive to NCAA basketball.

NCAA Tournament – a bracket style tournament of 65 teams to determine a national champion. Exclusive to NCAA Basketball.

NIT Tournament – the National Invitation Tournament is a 32 team bracket style tournament. The teams that play are not selected to the bigger, more heralded NCAA tournament. Often made fun of and dubbed the "Not Important Tournament" or the "Not Invited Tournament," the NIT still boasts great post season play. Exclusive to NCAA basketball.

Overtime – a five minute period of play at the end of the regular game (often called regulation) used to break a tie.

Paint – same as lane.

Princeton Offense – an offensive strategy that has the players moving around and passing the ball a lot. This offense slows the pace of the game and keeps the score low. It is often used when teams feel their opponent is more talented because it is often thought that a fast paced, high scoring game favors the more talented team.

Rebound – when a player gains possession of the ball after it hits the backboard or rim of the goal. Slang for rebounds is the term "boards." If a player has a lot of rebounds in a game, it is appropriate to say that he "crashed the boards" or "grabbed a lot of boards."

Red Shirt – a term used when a college player sits out a year. He is on the team but is not allowed to play in games. A red shirt year does not count against the player's four years of eligibility. Often times, a coach will red shirt a freshman athlete so that he can develop and grow more and still have four more years of eligibility after that first year. A player seriously injured before the season, or in the first few minutes of the very first game, will be given a medical red shirt so that they can heal and recover for a year and play the next year. A player that transfers from one D1 school to another D1 school must red shirt the first transfer year. (Unless the athlete transfers to another school in the same conference, in which case he would have to red shirt 2 years.)

Rookie – a professional athlete in his first season.

Set Offense – an offensive strategy that is a series of designed plays that can be written out in x's and o's on a chalk board.

Shot Clock – a clock that regulates the flow of the game so that one team doesn't hold the ball for an extreme amount of time. The clock resets with a change of possession or if the ball hits the rim of the basket. If the shot clock expires while the offense still has the ball, they automatically lose possession of the ball. In the NCAA, the shot clock is 35 seconds. In the NBA, the shot clock is 24 seconds.

Storming the Court – a celebratory gesture after a particularly big win where the students and fans jubilantly rush onto the court in mass quantities.

Taking a Charge – when a defensive player stands his ground as an offensive player runs into him on his way to the basket. The offensive player is hoping the defensive player will move out of the way. Taking the Charge is a move that can be perfected so that a foul gets called on the offensive guy whether it's a true charge or not. Defensive players learn to "flop" down on the ground at the slightest contact in hopes of drawing the foul.

Technical Foul – a foul that involves unsportsmanlike conduct, such as offensive language or excessive arguing, from a player or a coach. Technical fouls count towards a player's and team's personal fouls. The penalty for a "tech" is awarding the other team free throws as well as possession of the ball. Once a player receives two technical fouls he is ejected from the game. If a player on the other team is arguing with an official, it is appropriate to yell, "T him up, ref!" A team can also receive a technical foul if they call a timeout when they don't have any timeouts left to use. This was made famous when Chris Webber, part of Michigan's "Fab 5," called a timeout when they had none to use at the end of the 1993 national championship game against UNC. Michigan lost.

Tobacco Road – This term refers to the rivalry between the four major North Carolina universities (Duke, NC State, UNC and Wake Forest). Talk of games on Tobacco Road occurs almost exclusively when referring to basketball since all four schools have a history of impressive men's basketball programs. Duke, NC State and UNC are all located no more than 25 miles from one another. Wake Forest is located one hour west. The state of North Carolina has a history that is steeped in the old cash crop of tobacco and a legacy of college basketball.

Triple-Double – when a player records double digit statistics in three different categories.

Visiting Team – the visiting team is always listed first or on the top.

Zone Defense – a term used for a Defense that has each player on defense guarding a specific area, or zone, instead of a particular player.

The Pros: NBA Conferences and Divisions

Eastern Atlantic:
Toronto Raptors
New Jersey Nets
Philadelphia 76ers
New York Knicks
Boston Celtics

Western Northwest:
Utah Jazz
Denver Nuggets
Minnesota Timberwolves
Portland Trailblazers
Seattle Supersonics

Eastern Central:
Detroit Pistons
Cleveland Cavaliers
Chicago Bulls
Indiana Pacers
Milwaukee Bucs

Western Pacific:
Phoenix Suns
L.A. Lakers
Golden State Warriors
L.A. Clippers
Sacramento Kings

Eastern Southeast:
Miami Heat
Washington Wizards
Orlando Magic
Charlotte Bobcats
Atlanta Hawks

Western Southwest:
Dallas Mavericks
San Antonio Spurs
Houston Rockets
New Orleans Hornets
Memphis Grizzlies

The College Kids:

A quick note: College athletics is divided up into three major sections – Division I, Division II and Division III schools. Division III schools are typically private universities and do not give out scholarships to their athletes. Although they are the lowest division they do produce great players who make it to the professional ranks each year. Division II universities award scholarships and also have some reputable talent in the highest professional ranks: Ben Wallace of the Detroit Pistons played at Virginia Union.

D-I basketball is what where all the hype is. It is divided up in two sections, Major and Mid-major programs. Major programs are products of the largest power conferences and have the most money. Mid-majors are still very competitive, they just come from smaller conferences and tend to have lower budgets. Below is a list of some of the most prominent Major and mid-major conferences and schools.

Atlantic Coast Conference (ACC) – The ACC is made up of 12 D1 schools and has a reputation for being a dominant conference in men's basketball. The dominant rivalry is between Duke and UNC, followed closely by a heated rivalry between NC State and UNC in anything. Member schools: Boston College (BC) Eagles, Clemson Tigers, Duke Blue Devils, Florida State (FSU) Seminoles, Georgia Tech Yellow Jackets, Maryland (UMD) Terrapins, Miami Hurricanes, NC State (State or NCSU) Wolfpack, University of North Carolina (Carolina or UNC) Tarheels, Virginia (UVA) Cavaliers, Virginia Tech Hokies, Wake Forest (Wake or WFU) Demon Deacons.

Big East Conference – The Big East is made up of 16 D1 schools and is widely respected in both football and men's basketball. The World Wide leader often refers to this conference as the best from top to bottom. They are historically known for their Defense and athletic style of play. They have tough teams, with tough kids that you wouldn't want to come across in a bar room fight. Member schools: Cincinnati Bearcats, Connecticut (UConn) Huskies, DePaul Blue Demons, Georgetown Hoyas, Louisville Cardinals, Marquette Golden

Eagles, Notre Dame Fighting Irish, Pittsburgh Panthers, Providence Friars, Rutgers Scarlet Knights, St. John's Red Storm, Seton Hall Pirates, University of South Florida Bulls, Syracuse Orange, Villanova Wildcats, West Virginia Mountaineers.

Big Ten Conference – The Big Ten is made up of, you guessed it, 11 D1 schools and have been around the longest. It is made up of a lot of farm boys in gym shorts...they want to slow down the pace of the game and pummel opponents on both ends of the floor. Their reputation as a basketball power conference was sealed in the history books because of great schools like Indiana, Michigan and Michigan State. The "Fab 5" gained their fame as freshman at Michigan. Indiana basketball has a tremendous movie based upon one of their basketball seasons from decades past. You may have heard of it. It's called Hoosiers. Member schools: Illinois Fighting Illini, Indiana Hoosiers, Iowa Hawkeyes, Michigan Wolverines, Michigan State Spartans, Minnesota Golden Gophers, Northwestern Wildcats, Ohio State Buckeyes, Penn State Nittany Lions, Purdue Boilermakers, Wisconsin Badgers.

Big 12 Conference – The Big 12 s made up of 12 D1 schools that are really good at football. It's just how they grow 'em in that part of the country. Outside of Kansas, basketball is just something you do indoors to stay warm in between football seasons. Players and schools in Texas and Oklahoma have had some success on the basketball court, but Kansas rules the roost. They have dominated the national scene for decades. Member schools: Baylor Bears, Colorado Buffaloes, Iowa State Cyclones, Kansas Jayhawks, Kansas State Wildcats, Missouri Tigers, Nebraska Cornhuskers, Oklahoma Sooners, Oklahoma State Cowboys, Texas Longhorns, Texas A&M Aggies, Texas Tech Red Raiders.

Colonial Athletic Association (CAA) – The CAA has a great midmajor tradition. In recent years the University of North Carolina at Wilmington, or UNCW, Virginia Commonwealth and George Mason have been the dominant programs. GM made it all the way to the Final Four of the NCAA tournament in 2006, which is unheard of for a midmajor. Member schools: Delaware, Drexel, George Mason, Georgia

State, Hofstra, James Madison, UNC-Wilmington, Northeastern, Old Dominion, Towson, Virginia Commonwealth and William and Mary.

Conference USA (C-USA) – C-USA is made up of 12 D1 schools that often fly under the radar. These teams are often considered underdogs or "mid-majors" even though they are a part of a D1 conference. The only school to make some noise in the NCAA tournament in recent years has been Memphis. Member schools: University of Alabama at Birmingham (UAB) Trailblazers, Central Florida (UCF) Knights, East Carolina (ECU) Pirates, Houston Cougars, Marshall Thundering Herd, Memphis Tigers, Rice Owls, Southern Methodist University (SMU) Mustangs, Southern Mississippi (USM) Golden Eagles, University of Texas at El Paso (UTEP – pronounced you tep) Miners, Tulane Green Wave, Tulsa Golden Hurricane.

Mid-American Conference (MAC – pronounced mack) – The MAC is made up of 12 D1 schools that keep most teams on upset alert. Often thought of as mid-majors or underdogs, these teams often surprise their opponents and pull out a win. Member schools: Akron Zips, Ball State Cardinals, Bowling Green Falcons, Buffalo Bulls, Central Michigan Chippewas, Eastern Michigan Eagles, Kent State Golden Flashes, Miami (of Ohio) University Red Hawks, Northern Illinois Huskies, Ohio University Bobcats, Toledo Rockets, Western Michigan Broncos.

Mountain West Conference – The Mountain West is made up of 9 D1 schools that comprise the newest of all of the D1 conferences, having begun in 1999. Member schools: Air Force Falcons, Brigham Young (BYU) Cougars, Colorado State Rams, New Mexico Lobos, San Diego State University (SDSU) Aztecs, Texas Christian (TCU) Horned Frogs, University of Nevada Las Vegas (UNLV) Rebels, Utah Utes, Wyoming Cowboys.

Pacific Ten Conference (Pac 10) – The Pac 10 is made up of 10 schools and examined by the rest of the world for their strength in football. But, this conference boasts great basketball talent and tradition. They are known for their laissez-faire attitude on the court, the game is about style and finesse. It is also interesting to note Oregon's colors of green and yellow, as they make for some of the flashiest football uniforms to date. Pay careful attention to Stanford's nickname (Cardinal), as it is never plural. When the national media refers to USC, they are almost always talking about University of Southern California as opposed to the University of South Carolina. Member schools: Arizona Wildcats, Arizona State (ASU) Sun Devils, University of California Berkeley (Cal) Golden Bears, Oregon Ducks, Oregon State Beavers, Stanford Cardinal, University of California Los Angeles (UCLA) Bruins, University of Southern California (USC) Trojans, Washington Huskies, Washington State Cougars.

Southeastern Conference (SEC) – The SEC is made up of 12 schools that have fought to make a strong reputation on the basketball court. 50 years ago it was Kentucky and everybody else. Legendary coach, Adolf Rupp set the stage and the Jayhawks are currently the all time winningest team in the country. The conference has a reputation for heightened athleticism and spectacular plays. If USC is mentioned on a national stage, it is typically referring to the University of Southern California and not the University of South Carolina. Member schools: Alabama Crimson Tide, Arkansas Razorbacks, Auburn Tigers, Florida Gators, Georgia (UGA) Bulldogs, Kentucky Wildcats, Louisiana State University (LSU) Tigers, Mississippi State University Bulldogs, South Carolina (USC) Gamecocks, Tennessee Volunteers (Vols), University of Mississippi (Ole Miss) Rebels, Vanderbilt Commodores.

Sun Belt Conference – The Sun Belt Conference is made up of 13 D1 schools that are typically thought of as underdogs or mid-majors. Member schools: University of Arkansas at Little Rock Trojans, Arkansas State Indians, Denver Pioneers, Florida Atlantic University (FAU) Owls, Florida International University (FIU) Golden Panthers, University of Louisiana at Lafayette Rajin' Cajuns, University of Louisiana at Monroe Warhawks, Middle Tennessee State University (MTSU) Blue Raiders, New Orleans Privateers, North Texas Mean Green, University of South Alabama Jaguars, Troy Trojans, Western Kentucky Hilltoppers.

Western Athletic Conference (WAC – pronounced wack) – The WAC is made up of nine D1 schools. It is considered a mid-major conference, but seen to always pull off major upsets each year. Member schools: Boise State Broncos, California State University Fresno (Fresno State) Bulldogs, Hawaii Rainbows or Rainbow Warriors, Idaho Vandals, Louisiana Tech Bulldogs, Nevada Wolfpack, New Mexico State Aggies, San Jose State University Spartans, Utah State Aggies.

West Coast Conference (WCC) – The WCC is a small mid-major conference made up of eight schools. It makes the list because it's the home of one of the strongest mid-major teams in the country, Gonzaga. Year after year they have stellar seasons and always seem to pull off an upset or two in the NCAA tournament. Member school: Gonzaga, Loyola Marymount, Pepperdine, University of Portland, Saint Mary's, University of San Diego, University of San Francisco and Santa Clara.

Again, be aware that many teams share mascots. Tigers are claimed by Clemson, LSU and Auburn, to name a few. Wolfpack is shared by Nevada and NC State.

Again, be aware that some schools share initials. This is crucial knowledge because it's embarrassing to offer your thoughts about OSU if you're referring to Ohio State but the game on television is Oklahoma State or Oregon State. ASU is shared by Arizona State and Appalachian State.

THE SPORT: BASEBALL

Baseball is as engrained in our national history and as dear to our hearts as apple pie, thunderstorms, summer vacation, first love, catching lightening bugs and the Star Spangled Banner, something like that. It can be tough to follow baseball because they play more games than should be allowed in one season. Seriously, they play 162 games in the regular season. But, it's a good idea to pay attention to the highlights and the postseason. And, if for no other reason than because it's America's national pastime, choose a team to root for in the world series and pay attention to whether they win or lose. The whole season runs from the beginning of April until the end of October.

I grew up watching the Braves. Atlanta wasn't exactly close enough to hop in the car and catch a game every few weeks. We had to plan trips to go watch games in person. But, at every phase of my life, there have been minor league baseball teams that are good for a fun event. Trust me on this. Suggesting that you and your guy go catch a local baseball game is a great date idea. Even if he's not totally into baseball, he'll be impressed with your willingness to try something different. And it's a sporting event. If there's not a guy in the picture at the moment, organize a group of friends to head out to a local baseball game. A good mix of guys and girls are sure to have a blast sitting outside, socializing, partaking in hot dogs, beer, funnel cakes and, oh yes, the game. Invite your crush. He'll be impressed. It's a great event to mix things up and give people something new to do. One thing to know is that daytime games get really hot. Be prepared. A lot of minor league baseball games have special events or fireworks after night games. So do some digging and plan a great night out!

After college I moved to a new city that did not have a major league baseball team. But they did have a minor league team. A couple of folks from the group of friends I fell in with organized a bunch of us going to a night game, complete with post game fireworks. It was a great night and I still remember it clearly. I wore black capris, a white top, a red spring trench and black sandals. I felt cute and looked classic. Maybe I even looked too girlie for a baseball game. But, I could always make the excuse that I had come straight from work. I sat in the stands eating funnel cake with my new friends and ended up talking to Bank Guy. BG later admitted that it was an attractive combination that I looked 100% girlie, that I wasn't afraid to eat stadium food, and that I made off hand comments about baseball or sports in general a few different times in our conversation, all while being at a baseball game.

Major League Baseball season hits its stride during the summer months when there isn't a whole lot going on in the world of sports. Golf and NASCAR are good for some weekend entertainment, but baseball is really the only other live action that the media can focus on. It can be monotonous, redundant, boring, etc. Save for the college world series. Please know that I have no idea what goes on during the regular season of college baseball. But, come June, I tend to be starved for a new story in the sports world. Year after year, there's some feel good story about guys in the College World Series. Those stories and the games make for a new conversation piece during the dull summer months.

One summer, I went out several times with Beach Guy. It was new enough that we didn't have a title, talk every day, check in with each other's plans or spends days on end together. There was plenty of excitement and uncertainty. BG called to see if I wanted to hang out on a particular night. I said yes, and he proceeded to ask me what I wanted to do. Oh, the pressure of making that decision! I wanted to see BG, but I wanted to do something that he would want to do. I knew that his alma mater was playing in the college world series and suggested we watch the game. We had a great time! Would I have watched the game were I not with him? Probably not. It may have been on as background noise. But, because I knew BG was connected to one of the teams, and because I was into him, I made myself become more interested in the game. Please note that I am not a fan of his alma mater. So, my competitive nature came into the picture as I openly cheered against him and his team. More times than not, that is really fun to do!

The People:

Players – There are nine players in the field at one time for a given team. When a team is in the field, they are said to be playing defense as they are trying to stop the team at bat from scoring runs.

- **Pitcher (P)** – Typically, the most talked about player on the field, the pitcher's main job is to throw the ball to the batter. He also has to be prepared to field the ball and throw it to the necessary player if a hit is short and lands in the area around him.

- **Catcher (C)** – The catcher wears all of the protective gear since balls are being thrown at him and guys are swinging bats near him. He also signals to the pitcher what kind of pitch to throw to the guy at bat. The catcher protects home plate and fields any balls that are tipped or thrown in his area.

- **First Base (1B)** – The first baseman protects first base and fields balls that are hit in his area or thrown to him. He tries to get runners out at first base so they do not advance any further into scoring positions.

- **Second Base (2B)** – The second baseman protects second base and fields balls that are hit in his area or thrown to him. He can also start double plays by getting a guy out at second and then quickly throwing the ball to first so the first baseman can get that runner out, too.

- **Third Base (3B)** – The third baseman protects third base and fields balls that are hit in his area or thrown to him.

- **Short Stop (SS)** – The short stop lines up between second and third base. He fields balls that are hit in his area. He also helps cover second base when needed.

- **Left Field (LF), Center Field (CF), Right Field (RF)** – The outfielders catch balls that are hit in their area to get a batter out or to field a ball and quickly throw it in to the appropriate player. They must be able to run fast, have the expected hand-eye coordination and strong throwing arms.

The players above are considered to be the defense in baseball. They are defending the bases and home plate in order to keep the other team from scoring. The guys coming up to the plate to hit the ball are considered to be the offense.

The Words:

500 – a term used to indicate that a team has an equal number of wins and losses. This phrase was derived from looking at a statistics sheet where win-loss percentage was indicated as .500 meaning 50%. The goal for any team is to always be "above 500" for the season, which means that the team has more wins than losses. A team that is "under 500" is having a very bad year. Even just being 500 on the season is very mediocre.

Babe Ruth – one of the greatest players and biggest personalities of major league baseball. His 714 homeruns were thought to be a permanent record until Hank Aaron came along.

Ball – a pitch thrown outside of the strike zone and not swung at by the batter. A pitcher can throw three balls. Once a fourth ball is thrown, the batter automatically gets to go to first base.

Barry Bonds – holds the homerun record and the record for the most homeruns in a season (73).

Base Line – the lines extending from home plate down the first and third base lines into outfield.

Bases Empty – a term used to describe no runners being on any bases.

Bases Loaded – a term to describe runners being on first, second or third base at the same time.

Batter's Box – the area around home plate where the batter stands with his bat.

Batting Average – a statistic dividing the number of times a player has been up to bat by the number of times he has hit the ball. This is used to quantify how good or bad a batter is. A goal of .300 is typical.

Batting Order – the order in which offensive players lineup to take their turns at bat.

Bottom of an Inning – the second half of the inning. The home team bats during the bottom of each inning.

Bunt – a movement with the bat where the batter doesn't give a full swing at a pitch, but instead holds his bat out to just tap the ball onto the ground in the infield.

Bullpen – an area where pitchers warm up before they are called in to replace the current pitcher.

Cal Ripkin – holds the record for the most consecutive games played (2,632).

Catch – when a player in the field gets the ball in his glove after the ball is hit without dropping it.

Closer – a pitcher who is brought it at the end of the game.

Count – the number of balls and strikes a batter has at any given time. The number of balls is listed first and will be either 0, 1, 2 or 3. The number of strikes is listed second and will either be 0, 1 or 2. A 3-2 count means a batter has 3 balls and 2 strikes. This is considered a full count.

Cy Young Award – an award given to the best pitcher in baseball each season in the Major League. This award is selected by members of the Baseball Writers Association of America.

Defense – what is being played by the team in the infield and outfield.

Designated Hitter – a player chosen to bat for the pitcher.

Division – the three subsets of both the American League and the National League.

Double – when a batter hits the ball and makes it to second base in one play.

Double Header – two games in a row on the same day.

Double Play – when the guys in the field get two guys running the bases out in one play.

Dugout – where the members of the team sit when they are not on the field.

Earned Run Average (ERA) – a statistic for pitchers showing the number of runs without errors they allow.

Error – a bad mistake made on a routine play.

Extra Innings – the innings played if the game is tied after the standard nine innings.

Fly Ball – a ball that is hit high up into the air.

Foul Line – the lines extending from home plate down the first and third base lines into outfield. If a batter hits a ball on the side of those lines that is away from the infield or outfield, it is considered a foul ball. A foul ball counts as a strike, unless the batter already has two strikes. A foul ball cannot be strike three to get a batter out. However, someone in the field can catch a foul ball in the air to get the batter out.

Full Count – when a batter has three balls and two strikes. If a batter gets four balls then he automatically goes to first base. If a batter gets three strikes then he is out. A full count means there is one chance left to either get on base or go back to the dugout.

Grand Slam – a home run hit when the bases are loaded. A Grand Slam scores four runs.

Ground Ball – a ball that is hit onto the ground and rolls.

Hank Aaron – held the homerun record (755) until Barry Bonds broke it. Hammerin' Hank held the record for 33 years.

Home Run – a ball hit so far, usually out of the park in fair territory, that the batter gets to run around all the bases.

Home Team – the home team is always listed second or on the bottom.

Infield – the area around the bases and in towards the pitcher's mound and home plate.

Inning – a period of the game where both teams take turn being at bat and playing defense. There are three outs for each team in the inning. There are nine innings in a standard game. If there is a tie at the end of nine innings, the game goes into extra innings until one of the teams wins an inning to win the game.

Intentional Walk – when a pitcher throws four balls in a row to a batter so that the batter cannot swing at the pitches.

Inter-League Play – games between a team from the American League and a team from the National League.

Jackie Robinson – the first black major league baseball player. He debuted for the Brooklyn Dodgers on April 15, 1947.

Line Drive – a ball hit straight in the air right at a defensive player in the field.

Manager – the coach of the team. The manager sits in the dugout and wears a full baseball uniform like the players. This is the only sport where the coaching staff wears player uniforms.

National Pastime – the nickname given to baseball since it is the oldest American professional sport.

No Hitter – when the pitcher doesn't allow any batter to get a successful hit and get on base. Any pitch that may actually be hit will be caught by a defensive player or the runner will be thrown out before he reaches first base. A no hitter is an amazing feat by a pitcher and a tribute to the entire team's defense. Nolan Ryan holds the record with seven no hitters in his career.

Offense – the team at bat trying to score runs.

On Deck – refers to the next batter in the inning.

Out – the end of a play. A player is out if he hits the ball and a defensive player catches it before it hits the ground, if a defensive player tags him with the ball before he gets to a bases, if he swings for the ball and misses three times, if the pitcher throws him three strikes.

Outfield – the grassy area past all three bases towards the back wall and stands.

Pennant Race – the race between teams to win their league and get into the World Series.

Perfect Game – when a pitcher doesn't allow any batter from the other team to get on base at all. Perfection is a tough feat. There have only been 15 perfect major league games since 1900.

Pete Rose – holds the record for the most games ever played (3,562). But, he was banned from major league baseball for life because he gambled on the game.

Pinch Hitter – a substitute for a starting player.

Pitch – a ball thrown to the batter by the pitcher.

Pitcher's Mound – the hill in the middle of the infield from where the pitcher throws all of his pitches.

Pitching Rotation – the order in which pitchers start games. Usually there are several days of rest between starts for a pitcher.

Relief Pitcher – a pitcher that comes into the game after the starting pitcher.

Rookie – a professional athlete in his first season

Run – a point scored for the offensive team when a player makes it all the way around the bases without being called out.

Runs Batted In (RBI) – a statistic used to show how many times a player has been at bat and made a play that allowed other players to score runs.

Safe – making it to a base without being called out.

Scoring Position – a term referring to a runner on second or third base because he can score a run if the batter hits well.

Seventh Inning Stretch – a short break in between the top and bottom of the seventh inning.

Single – when a batter hits the ball and makes it to first base.

Starter – the starting pitcher.

Steal a Base – when a runner safely runs to the next base without the batter having hit the ball.

Steroid Era – the past few years of MLB have been covered in controversy surrounding players using performance enhancing drugs. Thus, the moniker was born to cover the times.

Strike – a call made indicating that the ball was thrown down the middle of the plate or that the batter swung at the ball and missed. A batter receives three strikes before being called out.

Strike Out – when a batter receives three strikes.

Subway Series – a term referring to games played between the New York Yankees and the New York Mets. Appropriately coined since all you need is a subway ride to get between the ballparks.

Top of an Inning – the first half of the inning. The visiting team bats during the top of each inning.

Triple – when a batter hits the ball and makes it to third base in one play.

Triple Play – when the guys in the field get three guys running the bases out in one play.

Visiting Team – the visiting team is always listed first or on the top.

Walk – when a pitcher throws four balls, the batter automatically goes to first base. Sometimes a pitcher will use a strategy where he will walk a batter on purpose by throwing four balls way outside of the batter's box. This happens if a batter is really, really good and tends to hit lots of homeruns. They would rather just stick him on first base than run the risk of him knocking one out of the park.

Wildcard – a spot in the playoffs given to a team that did not win the division.

World Series – the series of games between the best team in the American League and the best team in the National League to determine the baseball champion.

The Pros: MLB Leagues and Divisions

American League (AL):

AL East:
Baltimore Orioles
Boston Red Sox
New York Yankees
Tampa Bay Rays
Toronto Blue Jays

AL Central:
Chicago White Sox
Cleveland Indians
Detroit Tigers
Kansas City Royals
Minnesota Twins

AL West:
L.A. Angels
Oakland Athletics
Seattle Mariners
Texas Rangers

National League (NL)

NL East:
Atlanta Braves
Florida Marlins
New York Mets
Philadelphia Phillies
Washington Nationals

NL Central:
Chicago Cubs
Cincinnati Reds
Houston Astros
Milwaukee Brewers
Pittsburgh Pirates
St. Louis Cardinals

NL West:
Arizona Diamondbacks
Colorado Rockies
L.A. Dodgers
San Diego Padres
San Francisco Giants

The Others:

There are several minor league teams called "farm teams" for each major league team. The minor league teams have seasons similar to that of the majors. These farm teams are where players will go to develop their talent.

The College Kids:

College baseball isn't something that the majority of the population keeps up with. However, the College World Series can be a nice break in the summer monotony of regular season MLB, NASCAR and golf.

THE SPORT: HOCKEY

Hockey season starts in the beginning of October and lasts until the beginning of April. The playoffs start in April and conclude with the Stanley Cup finals in early June. The playoffs are comprised of eight teams from each league. The three division champions and then the top five points leaders from each conference make it to the post season. Each round of the playoffs is a best-of-seven series between two teams from the same conference. The finals of the playoffs are called the Stanley Cup finals. That is the trophy that everyone desires. It is not uncommon to find that players grow their facial hair during the playoffs because of superstition and tradition.

I became interested in hockey in 2002 when the Carolina Hurricanes, a recent addition to the North Carolina landscape, made it to the Stanley Cup finals. (Sadly, the Hurricanes lost in the finals that year.) During their playoff run, I was seeing a guy that was very into hockey. Knowing that I was interested in other sports, a friend took me to one of the playoff games. My very first hockey game. I loved it! The intensity was unlike anything I had experienced! Part of that was due to the fact that the Hurricanes were the supreme underdog in the playoffs and part of it was because a bunch of southerners (thousands) had continued beloved tailgating festivities with this new sport called hockey. But, the intensity is part of the genetic makeup of hockey. Regular season games may or may not be as intense as playoff games. That's typical of every sport.

Hockey has its fair share of differences. I had to learn them quickly. Being that I was a blatant bandwagon fan of the Carolina Hurricanes during their first playoff run, I had to get my act together so as to not look like a fool.

1. **Hockey players do NOT wear jerseys.** Who knew? In every other team sport, a guy wears a shirt with a name and a number on it called a jersey. That isn't the case with hockey. They wear sweaters. I guess they get cold on the ice. Or something.

2. **The Carolina Hurricanes used to be the Hartford Whalers until they moved to North Carolina in 1997.** In my early days of fandom, people would ask me if I had been with them since Hartford or if I was a Whalers fan. I would stare at them blankly having absolutely idea what they were talking about.

3. **The action on the ice is so very fast!** It is really hard to follow every single play, penalty, call, and aspect. Wow! I get worn out just thinking about it!

But, I did learn the general facets of hockey. Certainly well enough to watch with interest and follow along. I still prefer going to a game in person over watching a game on TV. Unless it's the playoffs. Then I'll take what I can get.

Regardless of how recently I became a fan of this thing called hockey, I'm grateful that I got to cut my teeth on the Carolina Hurricanes in 2002 because, then a seasoned fan, the tailgating in 2006 during our run in the playoffs was second to none. While most teams hail from cities too cold to sit outside and grill out from October to April, North Carolina has the distinct privilege (and determination) to tailgate any time for any sporting event. The truth is probably that we didn't know any better. We tailgate for every football game and for many basketball games. So why not tailgate for hockey? Right or wrong, I love it. Who else can say they tailgated (complete with grills, big screen television sets, beverages appropriately named "hurricanes," local law enforcement and tons of strangers) for the Stanley Cup finals? (Please note that the vast majority of said "strangers" are guys. Tailgating involved meat and beer and sports. There is nothing more manly than that.) And then we won it all.

But it doesn't end there. Following the Hurricanes win in the Stanley Cup Finals in 2006, players and coaches were greeting fans around town for weeks on end. Often times, they would be accompanied by the Cup. The Cup actually has bodyguards called "Keepers." They wear white gloves and travel with the Cup everywhere it goes. Emily Post would be proud. I want to be a Keeper of the Cup when I grow up. For real.

One evening I had an early dinner with some girl friends downtown. Walking back to my car, I was greeted by an acquaintance outside of a local bar and he asked me to join him for a drink. I politely declined. Nothing against Blue Eyed Guy. He was a very cute guy, had the most amazing blue eyes and I had met him a few times through mutual friends. But I didn't know him well enough to stay out by myself and have a drink with him. Plus, I was ready to get home because I had to get up early for work. Well, BEG pulled out a trump card when he informed me that the bar was actually closed for a private event for some of the Stanley Cup Champion Hurricanes players, coaches and guests, plus a few close friends of the owner of the bar. BEG was in. And so was I. I spent about an hour with BEG and met several players, as well as Lord Stanley's Cup. I even got to drink from the Cup. Germs are not even something that crosses your mind when given the opportunity to drink from a Cup of such tradition and legacy. I made my exit early enough to still have a normal bedtime and a great story to boot.

I had a couple of other encounters with the Cup in the months following the Hurricanes victory. It was almost uncanny how I would run into Stanley (my pet name for the Stanley Cup) when I was out and about or how I would be invited to attend events where Stanley was the guest of honor. But each moment with Stanley just made for a great story. And a lot of jealous guys.

The People:

Players – During normal play, there are six players, including one goaltender (goalie). These six guys play offense and defense. The five players other than the goaltender are typically divided into three forwards and two defencemen. The forward positions consist of a center and two wingers – a left and a right wing. Forwards often play together as units or lines usually with the same three forwards playing together. The defencemen usually stay together as a pair divided between left and right. Left and right side wingers or defencemen are generally positioned on the side on which they carry their stick. When one or more of these players get a penalty, they must sit out of the game in the penalty box and the team must play without them or a substitution. This means they are short staffed.

- **Goalie** – The keeper protects the net. He defends the goal from the other team scoring. In rare occasions, like at the end of the game when his team is down by one, he may be brought out of the net to play offense.

- **Center** – The center is a forward. As an offensive player, he skates around the whole rink but tries to get the puck into the net for a goal. A Center plays the middle of the ice between the left and right wings. He is often substituted in and out of the game with the wings, as the group of them may have great chemistry on the ice.

- **Wings** – The left and right wing players are forwards who play on either side of the center. They are offensive players who try to score goals. They are often substituted in and out of the game with the center, as the group of them may have great chemistry on the ice.

The Words:

500 – a term used to indicate that a team has an equal number of wins and losses. This phrase was derived from looking at a statistics sheet where win-loss percentage was indicated as .500 meaning 50%. The goal for any team is to always be "above 500" for the season, which means that the team has more wins than losses. A team that is "under 500" is having a very bad year. Even just being 500 on the season is very mediocre.

Altercation – physical contact between two or more players that results in a penalty.

Assist – the pass to the player who immediately scores a goal.

Attacking Zone – the space between the other team's blue line and their goal.

Backhand – passing the puck or shooting for the goal from the opposite side of a player's body. A right handed guy's backhand is from his left side and a left handed guy's backhand is from his right side. Backhand shots can be weaker than regular passes or shots.

Beat the Defense – the offensive player gets by the defensive players.

Beat the Goalie – they score a goal when the goalie is in the net by outmaneuvering him.

Behind the Net – the area of the ice behind the goalie's cage.

Blue Lines – the blue lines that run across the ice to break the rink up into three areas called attacking zone, defending zone and neutral zone.

Boarding – when one player forces another player into the boards. This is a minor penalty unless there is an injury, in which case it becomes a major penalty.

Boards – the walls surrounding the ice.

Body Check – when one player bumps or runs into another player with his hip or shoulder to make him lose his balance or to get in his way.

Breakaway – when one player has control of the puck and goes for the goal having gotten away from the other players and defenders.

Catcher – the glove a goalie wears on the hand without the stick.

Center Ice – the middle area between the two blue lines in the neutral zone.

Center Line – the red line across the rink halfway between the two goals.

Changing on the Fly – when players substitute for other players while the game is going on and the clock is running.

Charging – getting a head start with a few steps when going to body check another player. This is a minor penalty unless there is an injury, in which case it becomes a major penalty.

Check – contact made by the player without the puck to the player who has control of the puck.

Clearing the Puck – passing the puck all the way back to your own defensive zone to get it away from the other team and back into your own team's possession or when a goalie gets the puck away from the goal he is defending.

Cross Checking – using the stick to make contact with the other guy. This is a minor penalty unless there is an injury, in which case it becomes a major penalty.

Defensive Zone – the area closest to your own goal that you are defending from the other team.

Deflection – when the puck hits something (like a stick or a net or a skate) that makes it veer from a straight path.

Empty Net – when a team pulls their goalie out of the net to help in other parts of the rink.

Face Off – when a player from each team tries to gain control of the puck to start or restart play.

Forehand – passing the puck or shooting for the goal with the strongest side of a player's body. A right handed guy's forehand is from his right side and a left handed guy's forehand is from his left side. Forehand shots are usually stronger than backhand passes or shots.

Freeze the Puck – to force the puck against the boards with a stick or skate so it doesn't move and no one can play it.

Full Strength – when a team has all 6 of its players on the ice.

Hat Trick – when one player scores 3 goals in one game.

High Sticking – holding the stick above the shoulders to use against another player.

Home Team – the team listed second or on the bottom.

Icing – shooting the puck to the other team's goal from your side of the red line.

Line Change – substituting all of the players on the offensive line or defensive line at the same time.

Major Penalty – getting in trouble and having to sit out of the game for five minutes while the rest of the team plays. Teams may not substitute another player for the one who is sitting in the penalty box. They play with fewer players.

Match Up – the two players from opposing teams who are assigned to cover each other for the game.

Minor Penalty – getting in trouble and having to sit out of the game for two minutes. Teams may not substitute another player for the one who is sitting in the penalty box. They play with fewer players.

Neutral Zone – the area between the two blue lines.

Penalty – breaking the rules, getting caught and punished by having to sit out of the game for a certain length of time.

Penalty Box – the place where players who get in trouble go to sit out of the game.

Periods – a hockey game is divided into three periods that are each 20 minutes long. The periods are separated by intermissions.

Power Play – when one team is at full strength and the other team is short staffed due to one or more players being out of the game for a finite time for a penalty.

Rink – the area of ice surrounded by boards.

Sweater – the term used in hockey for the shirt or jersey the players wear. Perhaps the justification of that is that ice is cold so players must wear a sweater.

Stanley Cup – the cup itself is also known as the Cup, the Holy Grail and Lord Stanley's Cup. It is the team trophy that is awarded to the team who wins the Stanley Cup finals in the postseason. The cup was given by Lord Stanley of Preston in 1892 to be awarded to the best amateur hockey team. In 1915, it made its way into the professional ranks. The Stanley Cup awarded to winning teams today is that same cup. Only the original is passed to the winner each season. The names of the players of the winning team are engraved onto the cup each year.

Visiting Team – the team listed first or on the top.

Zamboni – the big machine that is used to clean and even out the ice during intermissions.

The Pros: NHL Conferences and Divisions

Eastern Conference:

Western Conference:

Atlantic Division
New Jersey Devils
New York Islanders
New York Rangers
Philadelphia Flyers
Pittsburgh Penguins

Central Division
Chicago Blackhawks
Columbus Blue Jackets
Detroit Red Wings
Nashville Predators
St. Louis Blues

Northeast Division
Boston Bruins
Buffalo Sabres
Montreal Canadiens
Ottawa Senators
Toronto Maple Leafs

Northwest Division
Calgary Flames
Colorado Avalanche
Edmonton Oilers
Minnesota Wild
Vancouver Canucks

Southeast Division
Atlanta Thrashers
Carolina Hurricanes
Florida Panthers
Tampa Bay Lightning
Washington Capitals

Pacific Division
Anaheim Ducks
Dallas Stars
Los Angeles Kings
Phoenix Coyotes
San Jose Sharks

THE SPORT: GOLF

The PGA Tour is the highest level of professional golf. The premiere players make it to the Tour. Golf tournaments are typically played Thursday through Sunday. It's only altered for special circumstances or holiday weekends. Round one is played on Thursdays, Round two on Fridays, Round three on Saturdays and the final round on Sundays. All scores are cumulative over all four rounds of golf. They player with the lowest score at the end of four days wins the tournament. If two or more players end with the same low score they will go into playoff holes to determine the winner. After the second round, the field of players is cut dramatically. Players that "make the cut" are those that play at or under than a specified score. (Remember that the goal in golf is a low score, so you have to be at or under the cut line to make the cut.) Players that are over the cut line score miss the cut.

The Tour season begins in early January each year with the Mercedes-Benz Championship in Hawaii. Only golfers that won tournaments the previous year are invited to play in this tournament. While there are tournaments virtually every week of the year, the "regular season" lasts until the middle of August. The PGA Tour began a "postseason" of golf in 2007. It's called the FedEx Cup. Golfers are awarded points after each tournament during the season. The number of points is contingent upon how they finish. The FedEx Cup playoffs are a series of four consecutive tournaments in August and September. Points continue to be awarded to golfers through the playoffs until a winner is determined. The winner being the guy with the most FedEx Cup points after the last of the four playoff tournaments. The first playoff tournament has the top 144 golfers in the point standings. The second playoff tournament has the top 120 golfers in the point standings. The third playoff tournament has the top 70 golfers in the point standings. The final playoff tournament has the top 30 golfers in the point standings and determines the FedEx Cup champion.

There are four tournaments each year that are considered "Majors." These four tournaments are the biggest tournaments of the year. Every golfer dreams of winning a Major. The Masters is always played at Augusta National in Augusta, GA in the spring (usually April) each year. The winner of the Masters gets a trophy, a lot of money and a coveted green jacket. The US Open is played in June each year at different courses in the US. The British Open is played in July each year at different courses. The PGA Championship is played in August each year at different courses in the US.

I'll be the first to admit it: golf can be really hard to watch on TV. Unless it's one of the four Majors or something especially intense is going on, it's easy to just check the leaderboard online to know all you need to know. This may sound awful, but a cold rainy Sunday afternoon is perfect for napping on the sofa with golf on TV.

Golf isn't a topic that comes up in general conversations as often as football, basketball or baseball. It's fairly easy to keep tabs on the golf world by being familiar with Tiger Woods and the big tournaments. Tiger makes it into virtually every conversation about golf in some way, shape or form. And sadly, the conversation is now not about his great skill at golf, but now it is about his personal failures.

While golf isn't the easiest sport to watch week in and week out, it sure can be fun to play. Or to try to play, anyway. There are plenty of guys who love to play golf, even if they don't watch it religiously on TV. Be aware that a lot of guys may want to use their time on the golf course strictly as time with other guys. They may even have a set foursome that they enjoy playing with. Let them have this time. Don't try to invite yourself along. Just like we need girl time to do our thing, guys need time to bond and just to be boys without us around.

But, golf can also be used as fun thing for you to do together. Every city has public par three golf courses that are fairly cheap and have casual settings. This may be way below your guy's skill level, but it's different enough from his typical outing with his buddies that it should make for a fun time. Many of those courses even offer specials like a bucket of balls and a bucket of beers for the driving range. Think of it kind of like putt-putt all grown up. Even if you're horrible at the game, it's still lots of fun! And you're sure to get points for planning an original, fun outing.

The Words:

Ace – a hole in one.

All Square – a term used to indicate that two players "in match play" are tied by having won the same number of holes.

Approach Shot – the play from the fairway where the next place the ball is supposed to land is on the green.

Back Nine – Holes 10-18.

Ball Marker – a small object used to mark where a player's ball has landed on the green.

Bare Lie – a ball lying on the ground with no grass underneath.

Birdie – getting the ball into the hole in one stroke under par.

Bogey – getting the ball into the hole in one stroke over par.

Bunker – an area of sand around the fairway or green that acts as a hazard.

Caddie – the person carrying a golfer's clubs. PGA Tour professionals are not allowed to use golf carts. Since they walk 18 holes, they each have a caddie to carry their clubs and help them analyze shots.

Chip – a very short stroke from just beyond the green to get the ball onto the green and rolling to the hole.

The Cut – in professional golf, after the first two rounds of golf (usually played on Thursday and Friday) a cutoff score is determined to narrow the number of players that continue to play. Players with scores higher than that cutoff "miss the cut" and are not allowed to play in the rest of the tournament. Players with scores lower than that cutoff "make the cut" and play the rest of the weekend for the cash prizes. Beginning in Round one of a golf tournament, it is every players goal to make the cut and then to go on to win the tournament with the lowest score.

Divot – a chunk of the ground that comes up after a player takes a stroke.

Double Bogey – getting the ball into the hole in two strokes over par.

Drive – a shot from the tee box that goes a long distance.

Driver – a wood that is used for long tee shots.

Driving Range – a practice area for tee shots.

Eagle – getting the ball into the hole in two strokes under par.

Even – being at par.

Fairway – the long area between the tee box and the green.

Front Nine – Holes 1-9.

Fore – something yelled as a warning to spectators if it looks as if the ball may land in a crowd.

Foursome – a typical grouping for casual golfers.

Green – the area where the actual cup and flag are on each hole. Players use their putters to get the ball in the hole from the green.

Handicap – a statistical calculation that makes every player equal in a tournament or round. This is not done on the PGA Tour or with other professionals. The higher the handicap, the worse the golfer. The lowest handicap is zero and is called being a "scratch golfer."

Hazard – bodies of water or sandtraps around fairways and greens.

Hole-In-One – getting the ball into the cup in one shot.

Hook – the ball sharply curving to the left (for right handed golfers) from a straight path in the air. This is not a good shot.

Iron – a golf club with an iron head.

Leaderboard – the scoreboard listing all of the players and the scores on each hole and overall.

Lie – the ground where the ball is. A lie can be good or bad. Good lies will be in the fairway or on the green. Bad lies will be in sand, the woods or the rough.

Match Play – a tournament style where two golfers play against each other and keep score differently than normal. Play on each hole progresses as normal. The player with the lowest score on the hole receives one point for winning that hole. The loser of the hole receives zero points. If the players have the same number of shots, they each get half.

Major – a really big tournament on the PGA Tour. There are four majors each year: the Master's, the US Open, the British Open and the PGA Championship.

Over – being above par.

Par – a term denoting the number of times a player has to hit the ball to get it into the cup on one hole or combined on all 18 holes. A hole on a golf course will be categorized as a par three, par four or par five, meaning that you have that many strokes to get the ball into the cup on that particular hole. An 18 hole golf course may be par 72, meaning that your strokes have to total 72 to be at par, or even, for the whole course.

Par 3 Golf Course – a public golf course that consists of only par three holes. These courses are considered to be casual and fun, and are cheaper to play than any other course.

The Rough – the grassy area around the fairway that is longer and not as easy to play from.

Sand Trap – a hazard area of sand around the green.

Scratch Golfer – having a handicap of zero.

Stroke – one shot.

Tee Box – the beginning place at each hole where the golfers take their first shots.

Under – being below par.

Winning – the lowest score in golf wins.

Wood – a golf club with a wooden head. These clubs are used for long tee shots. These wood clubs have been replaced with metal heads.

Woods – a really good golfer whose first name is Tiger. As this book goes to print, Tiger has announced he will return to golf after being away for several months. Tiger removed himself from golf for personal reasons. The entire sports world is speculating on what will happen to Tiger now. Will his personal failures affect his golf? Will he be as popular as before?

THE SPORT: NASCAR

The Nextel Cup Series is the highest level of racing in NASCAR. The premiere drivers race at this level. Nextel Cup races are on typically on Sundays, with the very occasional Saturday night race thrown in to shake things up a bit. Drivers get into a race by recording a time in qualifying that makes the cut. Qualifying is a couple of days before race day.

The NASCAR season starts in early February and lasts until mid-November with only a few weeks off during the year. It is the longest season in professional sports. In addition to prize money, drivers are awarded a certain number of points when they finish a race each week. During the regular season, these points accumulate. The regular season ends in September. At the end of the regular season, the 12 drivers with the most points are awarded spots in the Chase for the Nextel Cup. This is NASCAR's version of the playoffs. The last several races of the regular season are dubbed "the race for the chase" as drivers try to finish well in races in order to get more points so they can qualify as a top 12 points leader. The Chase for the Cup is 10 races. There is a full field of drivers for each of these last 10 "playoff" races, but only the 12 drivers that made it into the Chase are awarded points. At the end of the final 10 races, the driver from among the 12 in the Chase with the most points is the champion.

While races are held at different tracks throughout the year, there are a few tracks that are more famous than others. Bristol, Darlington, Daytona, Indianapolis, Lowe's, Pocono and Talladega are the speedways that are the most well known. But, Daytona and Indianapolis take glory and mystique to a whole new level.

It took me quite a while to get into NASCAR. It was on my radar as a sport because my baby brother Bo went to NASCAR school. (The kid is a genius – brilliant and so skilled at working on cars and racing them. Plus he's devilishly handsome. Go figure. Brilliant and gorgeous.) Anyway, I never really gave NASCAR much thought until the summer of 2004. Well, that's not true. I lived in Charlotte for a couple of years after college. Being that Charlotte is the mothership, the mecca for all that is NASCAR, I had gleaned information just by living there. And I watched on TV when Dale Earnhardt, Sr. crashed in the Daytona 500 in 2001 and lost his life. That was tragic. But, until 2004, I hadn't taken an interest in the sport for myself. I had listened to everyone around me and didn't have any opinions of my own on the matter.

In the spring of 2004, I met Preppy Guy. We began casually seeing each other and I quickly realized that, if he could always have his way, he would spend every Sunday after church watching golf and NASCAR. (Apparently, at the end of spring and through the summer, the only sports on are regular season baseball, golf and NASCAR.) This struck me as odd for several reasons. First of all, PG was the preppiest guy I have ever known. And wasn't NASCAR for mullets, jean shorts and wife beaters? The golf thing was easy for me. I was already interested in it. But NASCAR? I didn't have a desire to watch cars turn left for several hours in a row. Knowing that I have this little competitive streak in me, PG and I sat down one Sunday afternoon and he presented me with a challenge. PG told me that I could pick three drivers and he would pick one driver. The driver that finished best would be the winner. Doing simple math (three is greater than one), I took that bet. The loser had to buy the winner dinner at the winner's choice of restaurant. I chose three drivers based upon the color or the car, their names and how they looked. It was all very scientific. And I lost horribly. I don't think two of my choices even finished the race. But I was interested in the race and in the outcome. It held my attention and I cheered. NASCAR had its hook in me.

The next week, PG and I made the same wager. And I lost again. And again. Then I got smart. I liked other sports and paid attention to them. Why was NASCAR any different? I spent a little bit of time paying attention to the media and doing a little bit of reading online. The next week, when PG and I made out little wager, I won. And then I won again! I had quite the little win streak going. Just to tick him off, PG's dad called him and asked to speak to me, instead of his son, to ask for my thoughts on the race. I was tickled!

The People (as of 2009):

Number – Driver – Team

00 – David Reutimann – Michael Waltrip Racing
1 – Martin Truex, Jr. – Earnhardt Ganassi Racing
2 – Kurt Busch – Penske Racing
4 – Scott Wimmer – Morgan-McClure Motorsports
5 – Mark Martin – Hendrick Motorsports
6 – David Ragan – Roush Fenway Racing
7 – Robby Gordon – Robby Gordon Motorsports
07 – Casey Mears – Richard Childress Racing
08 – Terry Labonte – Carter/Simo Racing
9 – Kasey Kahne – Richard Petty Motorsports
09 – Brad Keselowski – Phoenix Racing
11 – Denny Hamlin – Joe Gibbs Racing
12 – David Stremme – Penske Racing
14 – Tony Stewart – Stewart-Haas Racing
16 – Greg Biffle – Roush Fenway Racing
17 – Matt Kenseth – Roush Fenway Racing
18 – Kyle Busch – Joe Gibbs Racing
19 – Elliott Sadler – Gillett Evernham Motorsports
20 – Joey Logano – Joe Gibbs Racing
21 – David Gilliland – Wood Brothers Racing
24 – Jeff Gordon – Hendrick Motorsports
26 – Jamie McMurray – Roush Fenway Racing
29 – Kevin Harvick – Richard Childress Racing
31 – Jeff Burton – Richard Childress Racing
33 – Clint Bowyer – Richard Childress Racing

34 – John Andretti – Front Row Sports
36 – Patrick Carpentier – Tommy Baldwin Racing
37 – Tony Raines – M&J Motorsports
39 – Ryan Newman – Stewart-Haas Racing
41 – J.J. Yeley – Mayfield Motorsports
42 – Juan Pablo Montoya – Earnhardt Ganassi Racing
43 – Reed Sorenson – Richard Petty Motorsports
44 – A.J. Allmendinger – Richard Petty Motorsports
48 – Jimmie Johnson – Hendrick Motorsports
51 – Dexter Bean – BlackJack Racing
55 – Michael Waltrip – Michael Waltrip Racing
60 – James Hylton – Carter/Simo Racing
64 – Mike Wallace – Gunselman Motorsports
66 – Dave Blaney – Prism Motorsports
73 – Mike Garvey – H&S Motorsports
77 – Sam Hornish Jr. – Penske Racing
78 – Regan Smith – Furniture Row Racing
82 – Scott Speed – Red Bull Racing
83 – Brian Vickers – Red Bull Racing
88 – Dale Earnhardt Jr. – Hendrick Motorsports
96 – Bobby Labonte – Hall of Fame Racing
98 – Paul Menard – Yates Racing
99 – Carl Edwards – Roush Fenway Racing
102 – Brandon Ash – Brandon Ash Racing
106 – Trevor Boys – Boys Will Be Boys Racing
113 – Max Papis – Germain Racing
127 – Ted Christopher – Kirk Shelmerdine Racing
146 – Carl Long – Carl Long Racing
157 – Norm Benning – Norm Benning Racing
170 – Andy Lally – TRG Motorsports
171 – Mike Bliss – TRG Motorsports
175 – Derrike Cope – Cope/Keller Racing
187 – Joe Nemechek – NEMCO Motorsports
204 – P.J. Jones – Robby Gordon Motorsports

The Words:

Backstretch – the long part of the track on the opposite side of the start/finish line.

Blocking – strategically positioning the car so that other drivers cannot pass.

Budweiser Shootout – a "fun" race that doesn't count for the points total that includes pole sitters from the year before and past Shootout winners.

Bump Draft – when a car right behind another taps the front car a little bit to make both cars go a little faster. While both cars do speed up a bit, this maneuver can get out of control very easily, especially in lots of traffic.

Busch Series – a NASCAR division that is a step below the Nextel circuit. Similar to a minor league, many drivers prove themselves in the Busch Series. Some Nextel drivers will race in a Busch Series race the day before the Nextel Cup race in order to practice or win.

Charlotte, NC – the Charlotte area, including Lake Norman, Concord and Mooresville, is accepted as the racing capital.

Checkered Flag – the race is over.

Chute – another term for a straightaway.

Crew Chief – the person in charge of the pit crew and the driver's strategy. He's kind of like the coach.

DNF – did not finish the race.

DNQ – did not qualify for the race.

DNS – did not start the race.

Drafting – one car riding directly behind another car very closely so that the front car gets most of the drag. This allows the second car to ride faster than normal.

Drag – resistance to air and wind caused from going so fast.

Field – the whole group of cars and drivers in any given race.

Firewall – the piece of metal that separates the engine area from the driver's area in a car.

Flagman – the guy that waves the flags to signal drivers throughout the race.

Frontstretch – the long part of the track that contains the start/finish line.

Green Flag – start or restart.

Handling – a car's performance. It's appropriate to ask how a certain car is handling.

Infield – the area in the middle of the track.

Intermediate Track – a race track that is between one mile and two miles in length.

Interval – the space between two cars referred to in seconds (or fractions of seconds) or car lengths.

Lap – once around the race track. If the lead driver has passed a car by more than once around the track, that driver has been "lapped."

Lead Lap – the lap that the driver in the lead is on. Drivers down a lap or more have been lapped by the lead driver and are not on the lead lap.

Loose – when the car feels out of control and like the backend may slip away into a fishtail.

NASCAR – National Association for Stock Car Auto Racing.

Nextel Cup – the top league in NASCAR with the famous drivers and highest winnings.

Owner – the person or group that owns the car and entire team. The owner takes care of the business aspect of racing, including sponsorship.

Pit Crew – the seven people that service a car when it is on pit road. They will give the car gas, change the tires, and do whatever else the car needs done in just a few seconds.

Pit Road – the strip of road just off the main track where the cars are serviced.

Pit Stop – when a car pulls off the main race track to get gas or new tires. This is often shortened to just "pit."

Pole – the first spot at the beginning of the race. The driver with the fastest qualifying time wins the pole.

Qualify – a time trial where drivers race two full laps at top speed a day or two before the Nextel Cup race. Only a certain number of the top drivers make it into the race. How a driver does in qualifying determines where he starts the race.

Red Flag – all drivers stop driving.

Restrictor Plate – and piece of aluminum in the engine that reduces horsepower and speed. A few races each year are "restrictor plate races" and have lower speeds than regular races.

Road Course – a race track with left and right turns at varying configurations. There are only a few road courses.

Roll Cage – the bars and pads that surrounds and protects the driver in the car.

Short Track – a race track that is less than one mile around.

Sponsors – the companies that pay to have their names and logos on the car and apparel of certain drivers.

Straightaway – the long straight parts of the track that don't curve.

Super Speedway – a race track that is two miles or more around.

Victory Lane – where the winning car parks after a race.

White Flag – one lap to go. The white flag is waved as the lead car enters the last lap.

Wide Open – when the driver has the petal to the metal.

Yellow Flag – caution flag.

THE SPORT: TENNIS

Roger Federer is the greatest tennis player of all time. That is all anyone needs to know about that.

THE SPORT: SOCCER

Don't even worry about it. It's not worth it. Seriously.

Now don't go get all huffy and offended. The point of this whole thing is to learn how to talk about sports, to become interested in sports. Soccer is a great game to play. Sign your kids up. Join a local rec league. Have fun with it. But learning the ins and outs of soccer so you can have a relevant conversation about it? Pointless. Unless you hang out in pubs with English or Irish guys, there is a very, very, very small chance that you will impress any guy with your knowledge of soccer. Very. They just don't care. I don't care. It's not worth the effort because the conversations will not take place.

The only thing I know about soccer is that some European soccer team traded David Beckham to a team in LA for over $120 million. And that David Beckham is WAY hot. (The only reason I even know that much is because it's all over every pop culture and gossip magazine.) As is some other soccer superstar named Ronaldo. But, I assure you that no guy will want to have THAT conversation with you. So skip it.

If you have to do something with soccer, play the game. Don't talk about it.

EXCEPT, and yes there is an exception to the above. If you are a girl living anywhere else in the world besides the good ole' US of A, you NEED to know more about soccer. And you can forget about most of the sports above because everywhere else in the world they eat, breathe, think and dream soccer.

THE STORY OF MY LIFE:

It was a Saturday morning at 9:30. My eyelids were still glued to my eyeballs. But not for long. Being that it was week two of the college football season, I had to (and wanted to!) be awake for College Game Day at 10:00. Kirk Herbstreit on TV is a wonderful sight to wake up to, let me tell you.

On this particular Saturday, however, I was woken up by my cell phone ringing over and over and over again. I considered throwing it across the room before I somehow managed the coherent thought that someone really must need to talk to me if they kept calling me at this hour. (It felt way earlier than 9:30.) I fumbled for the phone, very grateful for caller i.d., and greeted my caller with a hoarse, morning voice, mostly incoherent sound that resembled neither a "good morning" nor a "hello." It was my precious friend Brandi Baker who, while boasting a great stripper name, is not, in fact, a stripper.

"What's the lineup for today?" she asked in response to my morning voice mumblings. There was actually a sense of urgency in her voice. No small talk. No "good morning, sunshine." Nothing. She just jumped right in.

"Errrrrr…What do you mean?" I tossed out the general response because the only thing my two minute awake mind knew is that I couldn't make plans with her to go to the pool because I had 14 hours of football scheduled for the day. Seriously. College Game Day at 10:00. Nebraska vs. Wake Forest at 12 noon would be watched while saving seats at a local sports bar for the 2:30 NC State vs. Boston College Game. From there, I would be accompanying some friends to a different sports bar to watch the South Carolina vs. Georgia, UNC vs. ECU and Oregon vs. Michigan games. The nightcap was the much anticipated, early in the season top 10 matchup between Virginia Tech and LSU at 9:15. Now THAT is a good day. Football fun day is what I had affectionately dubbed it. And, boy oh boy, was I excited!

I assumed Brandi was calling to get me to soak up the rays, as had been our tradition for the previous 20 Saturdays. Believe you me; I am usually all about going to the pool. But, with the arrival of football season, my priorities had changed.

Brandi surprised me, though. She had not called for our weekly pool outing but, instead, had called to get the football lineup for the day. You see, Friend of a Friend Guy, her latest crush, loved football. He had taken her to the season opening NC State game the week before. Prior to the game, I gave Brandi a few helpful hints and talking points so that she would have something insightful and relevant to add to the football conversation and so that she would have some idea of what was being talked about all around her. FFG was impressed. Wanting FFG's approval of her sports knowledge to be legit, Brandi had called for more tidbits and nuggets about that day of football. And, not only did she want thoughts about the NC State game, Brandi wanted the lineup, background and highlights of the entire day in that, the second week of the college football season. She was hooked. I was tickled.

What had started out as a way to merely impress some guy had quickly, very quickly, turned in to actual interest on Brandi's part. It wasn't that she was, all of a sudden, the biggest fan or knew all there was to know. Instead, Brandi was interested in learning more about football because she finally was beginning to understand some of the things all the guys were talking about in their football conversations and she had added a couple of relevant comments the week before without being laughed at.

Brandi is just one example of how many of my friends became hooked on sports. So, turn on the TV, check out ESPN online, even read *Sports Illustrated*, etc. If for no other reason than impressing the guys or a guy. You never know , you just might actually find that you enjoy the game.

THE HOT TOPICS:

- **The BCS.** Does it accurately or fairly determine a national champion in college football? Would college football be better served with a brief tournament or playoff series? Universities often cite class attendance as a reason they don't support a playoff or tournament setup. But, would a playoff or tournament system interfere with class attendance since universities offer a break from classes for several weeks over the holidays? Is it accurate to say that money is the root of the issue and universities want the payout that comes from playing in bowl games?

- **Baseball and steroids.** Have all of the players used them? Should they be innocent until proven guilty? Is the court of public opinion too quick to convict? Should we just ignore it and chalk it up as being a phenomenon of the "steroid era?" Do records broken and set during said era need to be marked with an asterisk?

- **Coach Krzyzewski** (pronounced shuh-CHEF-skee). Do you love and/or respect the mastermind behind Duke men's basketball? Or has he shattered the dreams of your favorite team? Is he brilliant or overrated?

- **The Fed Ex Cup.** Is the PGA Tour's playoff system working? Does the guy with the most points at the end of the season really need the gigantic prize of $10 million?

- **Dale Earnhardt, Jr.** Do you love him or hate him? Is he riding the fame of his late father or has he come into his own?

- **Danicka Patrick.** What are your thoughts on women in NASCAR? I say – show those guys what a woman driver can do – you go girl!!!!!

- **Kobe Bryant and Shaquille O'Neal.** While there was much tension with them as teammates, were they better together than apart? Or has their split allowed for one or both of them to develop into better players? Are they right to bad mouth each other or should they just get along? Do you like and/or respect Kobe? Do you like and/or respect Shaq?

- **Tiger Woods.** Without a doubt, he is one of the greatest, if not THE greatest, golfers of all time. Do you love him or not? Do you cheer for him every weekend, root for the underdog or pull for his rivals Phil Mickelson and Vijay Singh? Do you like that he wears red and black every Sunday? Jack Nicklaus holds the record for winning 70 tournaments, 18 of which were majors. When will Tiger surpass Nicklaus and will he go on to completely shatter the record? Does he not have a stunning wife?

Sad Note: I wrote this before the scandal broke about Tiger's personal life. It is and always will be true that he is one of the great golfers of all time. But now, only time will tell how history will judge him.

- **Any underdog team that is doing well or pulling off a major upset.** Love the team or hate them, it makes for great stories and great conversation. Examples: Appalachian State beating Michigan in football in 2007, Stanford beating USC in football in 2007, Weber State beating UNC in the first round of the men's NCAA basketball tournament in 1999.

THE MOVIES:

To impress guys even when you're at Blockbuster.

Basketball:
- Pistol: The Birth of a Legend**
- Hoosiers*
- Blue Chips

Hockey:
- Miracle*
- Slapshot

Golf:
- Happy Gilmore*
- The Greatest Game Ever Played
- Tin Cup
- Caddyshack*
- The Legend of Bagger Vance

NASCAR:
- Talladega Nights*

Baseball:
- The Rookie*
- For Love of the Game
- Field of Dreams
- Bull Durham
- Major League

Football:
- Any Given Sunday
- The Longest Yard
- The Replacements
- Waterboy*
- Brian's Song
- Rudy
- We Are Marshall
- Remember the Titans
- Friday Night Lights
- Facing the Giants

*personal favorite

THE NICKNAMES:

Hank Aaron – Hammerin' Hank. Baseball player. Aaron embodies all that is class and character with baseball. He held the homerun record for 33 years.

Chris Berman – Boomer, the Swami. ESPN analyst. Berman has been a reporter and analyst for ESPN since just after their conception. He is famous for banter, wit and the nicknames he attaches to anything possible. High entertainment.

Jerome Bettis – the Bus. Football player. The Bus is power and strength and character and heart. He helped the Steelers win a Super Bowl.

Paul Bryant – Bear. Football coach. Bear Bryant is Alabama football. His name is synonymous with legacy and tradition.

John Clayton – the Professor. ESPN analyst. Clayton reports on and writes about the NFL for ESPN. He often goes head to head with Sean Salisbury on TV. Match ups between the Professor and the Quarterback are always enlightening and exciting.

Roger Clemens – the Rocket. Baseball player. One of the greatest pitchers of all time, Clemens, with seven, has won two more Cy Young awards than any other player.

Sidney Crosby – the Kid. Hockey player. Sid the Kid is one of the youngest players to ever become a dominant force in the NHL. He is not unlike LeBron James is to the NBA. Crosby was drafted for the NHL when he was 17 years old. Everyone wanted him. In his second season in the League, Crosby became the youngest player to win a scoring title. That same year, the Kid was the seventh player to win the three highest individual awards in hockey. He's the real deal.

Glen Davis – Big Baby. Basketball player. Big Baby made national headlines as a freshman at LSU in the NCAA tournament.

Joe DiMaggio – Joltin' Joe. Baseball player. DiMaggio played for the Yankees for 15 years and, at one time, had a hit streak for 56 consecutive games. He is also well known for his relationship with Marilyn Monroe.

Clyde Drexler – Clyde the Glide. Basketball player. Old school greatness.

Dale Earnhardt, Jr. – Junior. As a great NASCAR driver, Junior is called such because his father was a driver on the NASCAR circuit, too.

Dale Earnhardt, Sr. – the Intimidator. NASCAR driver. Earnhardt is also known for his number, 3. One of the all time great racers, Earnhardt lost his life in a tragic accident during the Daytona 500 in 2001.

Julius Erving – Dr. J. Basketball player. All that is basketball, Dr. J made the dunk popular.

Kevin Garnett – K.G., the Big Ticket. Basketball player. K.G. made a name for himself with the Minnesota Timberwolves.

Wayne Gretzky – the Great One. Hockey player. Gretzky's name is synonymous with hockey.

Ken Griffey, Jr. – Junior. Baseball player. It is often thought that Junior could be a contender in the all time home run race were it not for the injuries that have plagued his career. He plays with all out intensity and effort every time he is on the field.

Allen Iverson – A.I., the Answer. Basketball player. A.I. became a star playing for the Philadelphia 76ers.

LeBron James – King James. Basketball player. Coming straight out of high school into the NBA, LeBron made an immediate impact and has affected the game like few before him. He is heralded as being the next Michael Jordan.

Chad Johnson – Ocho Cinco. Johnson, who plays for the Cincinnati Bengals and wears number 85, has amazing antics and displays every football season. He talks a big game and backs it up on the field. Each time he makes a big play, he will entertain the crowd. Prior to one game, Johnson came out with his name on his jersey covered with his self imposed nickname "Ocho Cinco." It stuck. He legally changed his name to Ocho Cinco.

Randy Johnson – the Big Unit. Baseball player. Johnson is a great pitcher and made a name for himself with the Arizona Diamondbacks. He was traded to the Yankees and New York wasn't kind to him.

Michael Jordan – Air Jordan. Jordan became a superstar when, after great success at UNC, he played for the Chicago Bulls. He has an insane ability to leap from the free throw line and dunk a ball. Jordan's story is great because it is so rare. He wasn't good enough to play ball in high school. But, in college, he came into his own.

Mike Krzyzewski – Coach K. As the long time and very successful basketball coach at Duke, Coach K is called such because no one can pronounce is last name.

Pete Maravich – the Pistol, Pistol Pete. Basketball player. Pistol Pete was an amazing ball handler. It is said that he could dazzle crowds. In his college years at LSU, freshman were not allowed to play. So, in three years, well before the three point line existed (meaning players could only score one or two points with a basket since no basket alone counted for three points), the Pistol accumulated more points than any player in history. His record of 3,667 points scored in college stands alone and high above all others to this day.

Daisuke Matsuzaka – Dice K. Baseball player. It's good to have an easy nickname when your real name is hard to pronounce.

Tracy McGrady – T Mac. Basketball player. T Mac is a solid player who entered the NBA right out of high school. He is an all star and has led the NBA is scoring a couple of times.

Mark McGuire – Big Mac. Baseball player. McGuire briefly held the record for the most homeruns hit in a season.

Phil Mickelson – Lefty. Mickelson is a top player on the PGA Tour and is left handed.

Byron Nelson – Lord Byron. Golfer. Lord Byron was a dominant force on the PGA Tour in the 30's a 40's. His career is considered to have been brief. But, while brief, he did have one season where he won 18 tournaments, 11 of them in a row. Today, the PGA Tour honors Lord Byron by attaching his name to tournaments each year.

Shaquille O'Neal – Shaq, Diesel. One of the most dominating centers in the game, Shaq played for the Lakers before moving to the Heat.

David Ortiz – Big Papi. Baseball player. Big Papi plays for the Boston Red Sox and is a true power hitter.

Terrell Owens – T.O. or to (pronounced two, too, to and favored by Jim Rome). T.O. plays for the Dallas Cowboys.

Bill Parcells – the Big Tuna. All time great NFL football coach.

Chris Paul – CP3. Basketball player. CP3 was nationally known as a freshman at Wake Forest. He was a dominant point guard both years he played at Wake and then made the jump to the NBA where he made his mark as Rookie of the Year.

Walter Payton – Sweetness. Football player. Payton is remembered as being a great athlete who set many rushing records and a great man. He played for the Chicago Bears when they won Super Bowl XX.

William Perry – the Refrigerator, the Fridge. Football player. After playing at Clemson, the Fridge was drafted to the Chicago Bears and helped them win Super Bowl XX in his rookie season. At his peak, the Fridge was 6'2 and weighed in at over 325 pounds.

Andy Roddick – A Rod. Roddick is one of the top tennis players in the world.

Alex Rodriguez – A Rod. A Rod is one of the top baseball players in the nation. As of 2009, he is the third baseman for the Yankees and a candidate for MVP.

Ben Roethlisberger – Big Ben. Football player. Big Ben is the quarterback for the Steelers. He led the team to a Super Bowl win his second year in the league. I love him.

Sean Salisbury – the Quarterback. ESPN analyst. Salisbury is a former college and NFL quarterback. Currently, he reports on and writes about the NFL for ESPN. He is dubbed "the Quarterback" when going head to head on topics with John Clayton.

Deion Sanders – Primetime. Football and Baseball player. Sanders is one of the few athletes so talented that he was able to excel in the NFL and MLB. He is a human highlight reel.

Steve Spurrier – the Old Ball Coach, OBC or Darth Visor. Spurrier is the football coach at the University of South Carolina. Previously, he coached at Duke, had great success as the coach at University of Florida and a brief stint with the Redskins. He wasn't as successful in the NFL as he was and is in the college ranks. Throughout the years, Spurrier has worn a trademark visor during games. College football fans tend to love or hate the OBC. Darth Visor is a nod to the cap he wears on his head and is occasionally the name used by his foes as it correlates him with the head of the evil empire.

Craig Stadler – the Walrus. Golfer. Stadler has won several events on the PGA Tour and Champions Tour. He gets his name from his build and moustache.

LaDanian Tomlinson – L.T. Football player. L.T. is arguably the greatest active player in the NFL.

Mike Tyson – Iron Mike. Boxer. Tyson may be just as famous for his quotes and crazy antics as his boxing ability.

Dwyane Wade – D Wade, the Flash. Basketball player. D Wade was a monster player at Marquette and became an immediate role player at Miami.

Chris Webber – C Webb. Basketball player. C Webb was a member of the infamous Fab 5 at Michigan. He called a timeout at the end of a game against UNC in the NCAA finals when there weren't any timeouts left. The penalty for that was a technical foul. UNC won the game.

Carnell Williams – Cadillac. Football player. Cadillac played for Auburn and then was drafted to Tampa Bay.

THE NUGGETS:

Having a few surefire nuggets of trivia about sports is a necessity. Trivia makes great conversation in groups of sports fans.

During the summer of 1999, I worked at a camp in Colorado. I was sitting at a table having breakfast on one of the first mornings with one other girl and six guys. They were virtual strangers, but they were some of the people I would be living with and working with for several months. And one of the guys was really cute. I'll call him Surfer Guy. That morning, much to my pleasure, the guys started talking sports. Being that it was summertime; sports talk based upon current action was minimal. (Summer sports consist of regular season baseball, golf and NASCAR. But there is always trivia and general knowledge.) SG said he read an article in *Sports Illustrated* about how there are something like only 22 Division I schools whose nickname does not end in the letter "s." (For example, Clemson Tigers clearly ends in "s.") It was then that SG laid out the challenge: Who could be the first to name five of the schools? I had been pretty quiet in the sports talk up to that point. It was morning time, after all. They had no idea what they were in for. I smiled on the inside. I chewed and swallowed a bite of cereal, put down my spoon and said, and I quote, "NC State Wolfpack, Notre Dame Fighting Irish, Illinois Fighting Illini, Syracuse Orange, Alabama Crimson Tide" and continued eating my cereal. According to SG, it was then, exactly at that moment, that he fell for me. It was that powerful. We were inseparable for the rest of the summer.

Sometimes I'm not so knowledgeable. Sometimes it is the guy who greatly impresses me. A few years ago I was at a St. Patrick's Day party when college basketball came up in conversation. I can hold my own with college basketball talk and Runner Guy noticed. We worked our way to the outskirts of the gathering so that we could talk without having to fight the roar of the crowd. We covered a multitude of topics, but kept coming back to basketball. Finally RG did it. He pulled out all the stops. RG informed me that he knew every NCAA men's basketball champion since in all began in 1939. I laughed at him. Who, in their right mind, would take the time to memorize every national champion in men's college basketball since 1939? I teased the poor guy incessantly. We finally went inside and found a computer amidst the people. He pulled up some website and stepped aside. I sat down so that I could check his work. RG proceeded to recite every single college basketball champion since the beginning of time. I was extremely impressed. And jealous. It became my mission to learn the same feat. And I did it. All because some guy impressed me with his parlor trick.

Strangely enough, memorizing all of those men's NCAA basketball champions has come in handy a time or two. One night I was with some friends at a local pub after work for trivia night. This was general trivia without a specific focus on sports. My girlfriends and I invited a couple of guys to join us. About halfway through the 20 questions, the announcer asked, "Who won the men's NCAA basketball championship in 1939?" Well, duh. Oregon. It was the first team on a long list that I had learned just because some guy (ah yes…the infamous Runner Guy) had impressed me at a party years before. Without asking any of us, one of the new guys who joined us wrote down UCLA as the answer to the trivia question. It was a valid guess. Really. But wrong. I asked him what he wrote and he told us. My girlfriends, knowing my love for sports and the latest list of knowledge in my arsenal, then asked me what the right answer was. I told them all that Oregon won in 1939. They told the new guy that he needed to change his answer. After he continued to hesitate, one of the girls asked me if I would please recite all of the champions beginning with 1939. I didn't even have to start. The guy asked me if I really knew all of that and I was able to tell him yes, indeed. Thus began a great conversation. The girlfriend that I didn't know he had showed up not too long after that. She didn't like me very much.

Knowing little tidbits about sports doesn't have to be so blatantly obvious. During the summer of Surfer Guy, 1999, I proudly wore a

Weber State shirt. (The subtlety in this shirt still pleases me immensely.) Earlier that year, Weber State, a no name team from the middle of nowhere Utah, beat the dreaded UNC in the first round of the NCAA men's basketball tournament. It was, easily, the biggest upset of the year. Being a passionate NC State fan, I am required by the Code of Conduct to dislike UNC with everything in me. The day after Weber State pulled off the upset, I ordered Weber State apparel.

Wearing that t-shirt is my Cinderella's Slipper. It's not for everyone. Some people ignore the shirt because it means nothing to them. Some people may acknowledge the shirt to ask just where in the world is Weber State. But, there are a select few who see the shirt and understand that I am still so very proud that UNC went down in the first round to a determined underdog team in 1999. Regardless of their allegiance, there is a connection in the knowledge. A shared experience, if you will.

Division I schools whose nickname does not end in the letter "s":
Alabama Crimson Tide
Bucknell Bison
Cornell Big Red
Dartmouth Big Green
Elon Phoenix
Harvard Crimson
Hofstra Pride
Howard Bison
Illinois Fighting Illini
Marshall Thundering Herd
Massachusetts (UMass) Minutemen
Navy Midshipmen
Nevada Wolf Pack
NC State Wolfpack
North Texas Mean Green
Notre Dame Fighting Irish
St. John's Red Storm
Stanford Cardinal (never an "s" on the end)

Syracuse Orange
Tulane Green Wave (never an "s" on the end)
Tulsa Golden Hurricane
William and Mary Tribe (never an "s" on the end)

Schools without "college" or "university" in their title:
Naval Academy (Navy)
Air Force Academy (Air Force)
Virginian Military Institute (VMI)
Massachusetts Institute of Technology (MIT)
Georgia Institute of Technology (Georgia Tech)

Professional teams whose nicknames are in two different sports:
New York Rangers (NHL) and Texas Rangers (MLB)
New York Giants (NFL) and San Francisco Giants (MLB)
Arizona Cardinals (NFL) and St. Louis Cardinals (MLB)
Los Angeles Kings (NHL) and Sacramento Kings (NBA)

Teams that have never played in a Super Bowl:
Cleveland Browns
Detroit Lions
Houston Texans
Jacksonville Jaguars

The most Super Bowl have been won by the Pittsburgh Steelers with six. Next on the list are the Dallas Cowboys and San Francisco 49ers with five Super Bowls each.

The "Original Six" NHL teams:
Boston Bruins
Chicago Black Hawks
Detroit Red Wings
Montreal Canadians
New York Rangers
Toronto Maple Leafs

Montreal Canadians have won the most Stanley Cup Championships with 24.

The most NASCAR championships belong to Richard Petty and Dale Earnhardt, Sr. who each have 7 titles.

The first bowl game was the 1902 Rose Bowl, played between Michigan and Stanford; Michigan won 49-0.

Four college football stadiums seat more than 100,000 fans: University of Michigan, University of Tennessee, Penn State and Ohio State.

Appalachian State University is the only Division IAA team to ever beat a ranked Division I team in football. App. State beat Michigan who was ranked nationally at fifth on September 1, 2007. The game is heralded as one of the biggest upsets ever.

Tony Dorsett is the only football player to win a national championship in college football (with the Pittsburgh Panthers) and win a Super Bowl the next year (with the Dallas Cowboys). Dorsett also won a Heisman trophy. The additions of entrance into the college football hall of fame and the pro football hall of fame make him the only football player to have accomplished all five of those accolades.

Archie Griffin, who played at Ohio State, is the only player to win the Heisman trophy twice. Griffin won in 1974 and 1975.

University of Florida is the only school to win a national championship in basketball and football in the same year. Florida won the NCAA championship in basketball for the 2005-2006 and the BCS national championship in football for the 2006 season, making them the only team to win those two championships in the same calendar year. And when they were able to repeat as national champions in basketball by winning the NCAA tournament for the 2006-2007 season, Florida became the only team to ever win a football and basketball championship in the same school year.

University of Florida played Ohio State for the national championship in BOTH football and basketball in the 2006-2007 school year. This is the only time the same two teams have met in the national championship game for two different sports.

The "Fab 5" consisted of Chris Webber, Jimmy King, Jalen Rose, Juwan Howard and Ray Jackson.

THE WINNERS:

Super Bowl Winners (NFL – Professional Football)

I Green Bay Packers
II Green Bay Packers
III New York Jets
IV Kansas City Chiefs
V Baltimore Colts
VI Dallas Cowboys
VII Miami Dolphins
VII Miami Dolphins
IX Pittsburgh Steelers
X Pittsburgh Steelers
XI Oakland Raiders
XII Dallas Cowboys
XIII Pittsburgh Steelers
XIV Pittsburgh Steelers
XV Oakland Raiders
XVI San Francisco 49ers
XVII Washington Redskins
XVIII LA Raiders
XIX San Francisco 49ers
XX Chicago Bears
XXI New York Giants
XXII Washington Redskins

XXIII San Francisco 49ers
XXIV San Francisco 49ers
XXV New York Giants
XXVI Washington Redskins
XXVII Dallas Cowboys
XXVIII Dallas Cowboys
XXIX San Francisco 49ers
XXX Dallas Cowboys
XXXI Green Bay Packers
XXXII Denver Broncos
XXXIII Denver Broncos
XXXIV St. Louis Rams
XXXV Baltimore Ravens
XXXVI New England Patriots
XXXVII Tampa Bay Buccaneers
XXXVIII New England Patriots
XXXIX New England Patriots
XL Pittsburgh Steelers
XLI Indianapolis Colts
XLII New York Giants
XLIII Pittsburgh Steelers

NCAA Football National Champions (College Football)

1869	Princeton	1904	Michigan and Pennsylvania
1870	Princeton	1905	Chicago
1871	N/A	1906	Princeton
1872	Princeton	1907	Yale
1873	Princeton	1908	LSU and Pennsylvania
1874	Yale	1909	Yale
1875	Harvard	1910	Harvard and Pittsburgh
1876	Yale	1911	Penn State and Princeton
1877	Yale	1912	Harvard and Penn State
1878	Princeton	1913	Harvard
1879	Princeton	1914	Harvard
1880	Princeton and Yale	1915	Army
1881	Yale	1916	Cornell
1882	Yale	1917	Georgia Tech
1883	Yale	1918	Michigan and Pittsburgh
1884	Yale	1919	Harvard and Illinois and
1885	Princeton		Notre Dame and Texas A&M
1886	Yale	1920	California
1887	Yale	1921	California and Cornell
1888	Yale	1922	California and Cornell and
1889	Princeton		Princeton
1890	Harvard	1923	Illinois and Michigan
1891	Yale	1924	Notre Dame
1892	Yale	1925	Alabama
1893	Princeton	1926	Alabama and Stanford
1894	Yale	1927	Illinois and Yale
1895	Pennsylvania	1928	Georgia Tech
1896	Lafayette and Princeton	1929	Notre Dame
1897	Pennsylvania	1930	Alabama and Notre Dame
1898	Harvard	1931	USC
1899	Harvard	1932	USC
1900	Yale	1933	Michigan
1901	Michigan	1934	Minnesota
1902	Michigan	1935	Minnesota
1903	Michigan and Princeton	1936	Minnesota

1937 Pittsburgh	1971 Nebraska
1938 TCU	1972 USC
1939 Texas A&M	1973 Notre Dame and Alabama
1940 Minnesota	1974 USC and Oklahoma
1941 Minnesota	1975 Oklahoma
1942 Ohio State	1976 Pittsburgh
1943 Notre Dame	1977 Notre Dame
1944 Army	1978 Alabama and USC
1945 Army	1979 Alabama
1946 Notre Dame	1980 Georgia
1947 Notre Dame	1981 Clemson
1948 Michigan	1982 Penn State
1949 Notre Dame	1983 Miami
1950 Oklahoma	1984 BYU
1951 Tennessee	1985 Oklahoma
1952 Michigan State	1986 Penn State
1953 Maryland	1987 Miami
1954 UCLA and Ohio State	1988 Notre Dame
1955 Oklahoma	1989 Miami
1956 Oklahoma	1990 Colorado and Georgia Tech
1957 Ohio State and Auburn	1991 Washington and Miami
1958 LSU and Iowa	1992 Alabama
1959 Syracuse	1993 Florida State
1960 Minnesota and Mississippi	1994 Nebraska
1961 Alabama and Ohio State	1995 Nebraska
1962 USC	1996 Florida
1963 Texas	1997 Michigan and Nebraska
1964 Alabama and Arkansas and Notre Dame	1998 Tennessee
	1999 Florida State
1965 Michigan State and Alabama	2000 Oklahoma
	2001 Miami
1966 Notre Dame and Michigan State	2002 Ohio State
	2003 LSU and USC
1967 USC	2004 USC
1968 Ohio State	2005 Texas
1969 Texas	2006 Florida
1970 Nebraska and Texas and Ohio State	2007 LSU
	2008 Florida

Heisman Trophy Winners
(Award for the best player in college football)

1935 Jay Berwanger – Chicago – RB
1936 Larry Kelley – Yale – E
1937 Clint Frank – Yale – QB
1938 Davey O'Brien – TCU – QB
1939 Nile Kinnick – Iowa – RB
1940 Tom Harmon – Michigan – RB
1941 Bruce Smith – Minnesota – RB
1942 Frank Sinkwich – Georgia – RB
1943 Angelo Bertelli – Notre Dame – QB
1944 Les Horvath – Ohio State – QB
1945 Doc Blanchard – Army – FB
1946 Glenn Davis – Army – RB
1947 Jack Lujack – Notre Dame – QB
1948 Doak Walker – SMU – RB
1949 Leon Hart – Notre Dame – E
1950 Vic Janowicz – Ohio State – RB
1951 Dick Kazmaier – Princeton – RB
1952 Billy Vessels – Oklahoma – RB
1953 John Lattner – Notre Dame – RB
1954 Alan Ameche – Wisconsin – FB
1955 Howard Cassady – Ohio State – RB
1956 Paul Hornung – Notre Dame – QB
1957 John David Crow – Texas A&M – RB
1958 Pete Dawkins – Army – RB
1959 Billy Cannon – LSU – RB
1960 Joe Bellino – Navy – RB
1961 Ernie Davis – Syracuse – RB
1962 Terry Baker – Oregon State – QB
1963 Roger Staubach – Navy – QB
1964 John Huarte – Notre Dame – QB
1965 Mike Garrett – USC – RB
1966 Steve Spurrier – Florida – QB
1967 Gary Beban – UCLA – QB
1968 O.J. Simpson – USC – RB

1969 Steve Owens – Oklahoma – FB
1970 Jim Plunkett – Stanford – QB
1971 Pat Sullivan – Auburn – QB
1972 Johnny Rodgers – Nebraska – RB
1973 John Cappelletti – Penn State – RB
1974 Archie Griffin – Ohio State – RB
1975 Archie Griffin – Ohio State – RB
1976 Tony Dorsett – Pittsburgh – RB
1977 Earl Campbell – Texas – RB
1978 Billy Sims – Oklahoma – RB
1979 Charles White – USC – RB
1980 George Rogers – South Carolina – RB
1981 Marcus Allen – USC – RB
1982 Herschel Walker – Georgia – RB
1983 Mike Rozier – Nebraska – RB
1984 Doug Flutie – Boston College – QB
1985 Bo Jackson – Auburn – RB
1986 Vinny Testaverde – Miami – QB
1987 Tim Brown – Notre Dame – WR
1988 Barry Sanders – Oklahoma State – RB
1989 Andre Ware – Houston – QB
1990 Ty Detmer – BYU – QB
1991 Desmond Howard – Michigan – WR
1992 Gino Torretta – Miami – QB
1993 Charlie Ward – Florida State – QB
1994 Rashaan Salaam – Colorado – RB
1995 Eddie George – Ohio State – RB
1996 Danny Wuerffel – Florida – QB
1997 Charles Woodson – Michigan – CB
1998 Ricky Williams – Texas – RB
1999 Ron Dayne – Wisconsin – RB
2000 Chris Weinke – Florida State – QB
2001 Eric Crouch – Nebraska – QB
2002 Carson Palmer – USC – QB
2003 Jason White – Oklahoma – QB
2004 Matt Leinart – USC – QB
2005 Reggie Bush – USC – RB

2006   Troy Smith – Ohio State – QB
2007   Tim Tebow – Florida – QB
2008   Sam Bradford – Oklahoma – QB

NBA Finals Winners (Professional basketball)

1946-1947 Philadelphia Warriors
1947-1948 Baltimore Bullets
1948-1949 Minneapolis Lakers
1949-1950 Minneapolis Lakers
1950-1951 Rochester Royals
1951-1952 Minneapolis Lakers
1952-1953 Minneapolis Lakers
1953-1954 Minneapolis Lakers
1954-1955 Syracuse Nationals
1955-1956 Philadelphia Warriors
1956-1957 Boston Celtics
1957-1958 St. Louis Hawks
1958-1959 Boston Celtics
1959-1960 Boston Celtics
1960-1961 Boston Celtics
1961-1962 Boston Celtics
1962-1963 Boston Celtics
1963-1964 Boston Celtics
1964-1965 Boston Celtics
1965-1966 Boston Celtics
1966-1967 Philadelphia 76ers
1967-1968 Boston Celtics
1968-1969 Boston Celtics
1969-1970 New York Knicks
1970-1971 Milwaukee Bucks
1971-1972 Los Angeles Lakers
1972-1973 New York Knicks
1973-1974 Boston Celtics
1974-1975 Golden State Warriors
1975-1976 Boston Celtics
1976-1977 Portland Trailblazers
1977-1978 Washington Bullets
1978-1979 Seattle SuperSonics
1979-1980 Los Angeles Lakers
1980-1981 Boston Celtics

1981-1982 Los Angeles Lakers
1982-1983 Philadelphia 76ers
1983-1984 Boston Celtics
1984-1985 Los Angeles Lakers
1985-1986 Boston Celtics
1986-1987 Los Angeles Lakers
1987-1988 Los Angeles Lakers
1988-1989 Detroit Pistons
1989-1990 Detroit Pistons
1990-1991 Chicago Bulls
1991-1992 Chicago Bulls
1992-1993 Chicago Bulls
1993-1994 Houston Rockets
1994-1995 Houston Rockets
1995-1996 Chicago Bulls
1996-1997 Chicago Bulls
1998-1999 San Antonio Spurs
1999-2000 Los Angeles Lakers
2000-2001 Los Angeles Lakers
2001-2002 Los Angeles Lakers
2002-2003 San Antonio Spurs
2003-2004 Detroit Pistons
2004-2005 San Antonio Spurs
2005-2006 Miami Heat
2006-2007 San Antonio Spurs
2007-2008 Boston Celtics
2008-2009 Los Angeles Lakers

NCAA Men's Basketball Champions (College basketball)

1939	Oregon	1975	UCLA
1940	Indiana	1976	Indiana
1941	Wisconsin	1977	Marquette
1942	Stanford	1978	Kentucky
1943	Wyoming	1979	Michigan State
1944	Utah	1980	Louisville
1945	Oklahoma State	1981	Indiana
1946	Oklahoma State	1982	North Carolina
1947	Holy Cross	1983	North Carolina State
1948	Kentucky	1984	Georgetown
1949	Kentucky	1985	Villanova
1950	CCNY	1986	Louisville
1951	Kentucky	1987	Indiana
1952	Kansas	1988	Kansas
1953	Indiana	1989	Michigan
1954	La Salle	1990	UNLV
1955	San Francisco	1991	Duke
1956	San Francisco	1992	Duke
1957	North Carolina	1993	North Carolina
1958	Kentucky	1994	Arkansas
1959	California	1995	UCLA
1960	Ohio State	1996	Kentucky
1961	Cincinnati	1997	Arizona
1962	Cincinnati	1998	Kentucky
1963	Loyola	1999	Connecticut
1964	UCLA	2000	Michigan State
1965	UCLA	2001	Duke
1966	UTEP	2002	Maryland
1967	UCLA	2003	Syracuse
1968	UCLA	2004	Connecticut
1969	UCLA	2005	North Carolina
1970	UCLA	2006	Florida
1971	UCLA	2007	Florida
1972	UCLA	2008	Kansas
1973	UCLA	2009	North Carolina
1974	NC State		

Baseball World Series Winners (MLB – Professional baseball)

1903	Boston Pilgrims	1938	New York Yankees
1904	N/A	1939	New York Yankees
1905	New York Giants	1940	Cincinnati Reds
1906	Chicago White Sox	1941	New York Yankees
1907	Chicago Cubs	1942	St. Louis Cardinals
1908	Chicago Cubs	1943	New York Yankees
1909	Pittsburgh Pirates	1944	St. Louis Cardinals
1910	Philadelphia Athletics	1945	Detroit Tigers
1911	Philadelphia Athletics	1946	St. Louis Cardinals
1912	Boston Red Sox	1947	New York Yankees
1913	Philadelphia Athletics	1948	Cleveland Indians
1914	Boston Braves	1949	New York Yankees
1915	Boston Red Sox	1950	New York Yankees
1916	Boston Red Sox	1951	New York Yankees
1917	Chicago White Sox	1952	New York Yankees
1918	Boston Red Sox	1953	New York Yankees
1919	Cincinnati Reds	1954	New York Giants
1920	Cleveland Indians	1955	Brooklyn Dodgers
1921	New York Giants	1956	New York Yankees
1922	New York Giants	1957	Milwaukee Braves
1923	New York Yankees	1958	New York Yankees
1924	Washington Senators	1959	Los Angeles Dodgers
1925	Pittsburgh Pirates	1960	Pittsburgh Pirates
1926	St. Louis Cardinals	1961	New York Yankees
1927	New York Yankees	1962	New York Yankees
1928	New York Yankees	1963	Los Angeles Dodgers
1929	Philadelphia Athletics	1964	St. Louis Cardinals
1930	Philadelphia Athletics	1965	Los Angeles Dodgers
1931	St. Louis Cardinals	1966	Baltimore Orioles
1932	New York Yankees	1967	St. Louis Cardinals
1933	New York Giants	1968	Detroit Tigers
1934	St. Louis Cardinals	1969	New York Mets
1935	Detroit Tigers	1970	Baltimore Orioles
1936	New York Yankees	1971	Pittsburgh Pirates
1937	New York Yankees	1972	Oakland Athletics

1973 Oakland Athletics
1974 Oakland Athletics
1975 Cincinnati Reds
1976 Cincinnati Reds
1977 New York Yankees
1978 New York Yankees
1979 Pittsburgh Pirates
1980 Philadelphia Phillies
1981 Los Angeles Dodgers
1982 St. Louis Cardinals
1983 Baltimore Orioles
1984 Detroit Tigers
1985 Kansas City Royals
1986 New York Mets
1987 Minnesota Twins
1988 Los Angeles Dodgers
1989 Oakland Athletics
1990 Cincinnati Reds
1991 Minnesota Twins
1992 Toronto Blue Jays
1993 Toronto Blue Jays
1994 N/A
1995 Atlanta Braves
1996 New York Yankees
1997 Florida Marlins
1998 New York Yankees
1999 New York Yankees
2000 New York Yankees
2001 Arizona Diamondbacks
2002 Anaheim Angels
2003 Florida Marlins
2004 Boston Red Sox
2005 Chicago White Sox
2006 St. Louis Cardinals
2007 Boston Red Sox
2008 Philadelphia Phillies

Stanley Cup Winners (Professional hockey)

1892-1893 Montreal Amateur Athletic Association (AAA)
1893-1894 Montreal AAA
1894-1895 Montreal Victorias
1895-1896 Montreal Victorias
1895-1896 Winnipeg Victorias
1896-1897 Montreal Victorias
1897-1898 Montreal Victorias
1898-1899 Montreal Shamrocks
1899-1900 Montreal Shamrocks
1900-1901 Winnipeg Victoria
1901-1902 Montreal AAA
1901-1902 Winnipeg Victoria
1902-1903 Montreal AAA
1902-1903 Ottawa Senators
1903-1904 Ottawa Senators
1904-1905 Ottawa Senators
1905-1906 Montreal Wanderers
1905-1906 Ottawa Senators
1906-1907 Kenora Thistles
1906-1907 Montreal Wanderers
1907-1908 Montreal Wanderers
1908-1909 Ottawa Senators
1909-1910 Montreal Wanderers
1910-1911 Ottawa Senators
1911-1912 Quebec Bulldogs
1912-1923 Quebec Bulldogs
1913-1914 Toronto Blueshirts
1914-1915 Vancouver Millionaires
1915-1916 Montreal Canadians
1916-1917 Seattle Metropolitians
1917-1918 Toronto Arenas
1918-1919 No decision
1919-1920 Ottawa Senators
1920-1921 Ottawa Senators
1921-1922 Toronto St. Pats

1922-1923 Ottawa Senators
1923-1924 Montreal Canadians
1924-1925 Victoria Cougars
1925-1926 Montreal Maroons
1926-1927 Ottawa Senators
1927-1928 New York Rangers
1928-1929 Boston Bruins
1929-1930 Montreal Canadians
1930-1931 Montreal Canadians
1931-1932 Toronto Maple Leafs
1932-1933 New York Rangers
1933-1934 Chicago Black Hawks
1934-1935 Montreal Maroons
1935-1936 Detroit Red Wings
1936-1937 Detroit Red Wings
1937-1938 Chicago Black Hawks
1938-1939 Boston Bruins
1939-1940 New York Rangers
1940-1941 Boston Bruins
1941-1942 Toronto Maple Leafs
1942-1943 Detroit Red Wings
1943-1944 Montreal Canadians
1944-1945 Toronto Maple Leafs
1945-1946 Montreal Canadians
1946-1947 Toronto Maple Leafs
1947-1948 Toronto Maple Leafs
1948-1949 Toronto Maple Leafs
1949-1950 Detroit Red Wings
1950-1951 Toronto Maple Leafs
1951-1952 Detroit Red Wings
1952-1953 Montreal Canadians
1953-1954 Detroit Red Wings
1954-1955 Detroit Red Wings
1955-1956 Montreal Canadians
1956-1957 Montreal Canadians
1957-1958 Montreal Canadians
1958-1959 Montreal Canadians

1959-1960 Montreal Canadians
1960-1961 Chicago Blackhawks
1961-1962 Toronto Maple Leafs
1962-1963 Toronto Maple Leafs
1963-1964 Toronto Maple Leafs
1964-1965 Montreal Canadians
1965-1966 Montreal Canadians
1966-1967 Toronto Maple Leafs
1967-1968 Montreal Canadians
1968-1969 Montreal Canadians
1969-1970 Boston Bruins
1970-1971 Montreal Canadians
1971-1972 Boston Bruins
1972-1973 Montreal Canadians
1973-1974 Philadelphia Flyers
1974-1975 Philadelphia Flyers
1975-1976 Montreal Canadians
1976-1977 Montreal Canadians
1977-1978 Montreal Canadians
1978-1979 Montreal Canadians
1979-1980 New York Islanders
1980-1981 New York Islanders
1981-1982 New York Islanders
1982-1983 New York Islanders
1983-1984 Edmonton Oilers
1984-1985 Edmonton Oilers
1985-1986 Montreal Canadians
1986-1987 Edmonton Oilers
1987-1988 Edmonton Oilers
1988-1989 Calgary Flames
1989-1990 Edmonton Oilers
1990-1991 Pittsburgh Penguins
1991-1992 Pittsburgh Penguins
1992-1993 Montreal Canadians
1993-1994 New York Rangers
1994-1995 New Jersey Devils
1995-1996 Colorado Avalanche

1996-1997 Detroit Red Wings
1997-1998 Detroit Red Wings
1998-1999 Dallas Stars
1999-2000 New Jersey Devils
2000-2001 Colorado Avalanche
2001-2002 Detroit Red Wings
2002-2003 New Jersey Devils
2003-2004 Tampa Bay Lightning
2004-2005 N/A
2005-2006 Carolina Hurricanes
2006-2007 Anaheim Ducks
2007-2008 Detroit Red Wings
2008-2009 Pittsburgh Penguins

Masters Winners (PGA Tour golf – one of the four Majors)

1934	Horton Smith	1969	George Archer
1935	Gene Sarazen	1970	Billy Casper
1936	Horton Smith	1971	Charles Coody
1937	Byron Nelson	1972	Jack Nicklaus
1938	Henry Picard	1973	Tommy Aaron
1939	Ralph Guldahl	1974	Gary Player
1940	Jimmy Demaret	1975	Jack Nicklaus
1941	Craig Wood	1976	Raymond Floyd
1942	Byron Nelson	1977	Tom Watson
1943	WW II	1978	Gary Player
1944	WW II	1979	Fuzzy Zoeller
1945	WW II	1980	Steve Ballesteros
1946	Herman Keiser	1981	Tom Watson
1947	Jimmy Demaret	1982	Craig Stadler
1948	Claude Harmon	1983	Steve Ballesteros
1949	Sam Snead	1984	Ben Crenshaw
1950	Jimmy Demaret	1985	Bernhard Langer
1951	Ben Hogan	1986	Jack Nicklaus
1952	Sam Snead	1987	Larry Mize
1953	Ben Hogan	1988	Sandy Lyle
1954	Sam Snead	1989	Nick Faldo
1955	Cary Middlecoff	1990	Nick Faldo
1956	Jack Burke, Jr.	1991	Iam Woosnam
1957	Doug Ford	1992	Fred Couples
1958	Arnold Palmer	1993	Bernhard Langer
1959	Art Wall, Jr.	1994	Jose Maria Olazabal
1960	Arnold Palmer	1995	Ben Crenshaw
1961	Gary Player	1996	Nick Faldo
1962	Arnold Palmer	1997	Tiger Woods
1963	Jack Nicklaus	1998	Mark O'Meara
1964	Arnold Palmer	1999	Jose Maria Olazabal
1965	Jack Nicklaus	2000	Vijay Singh
1966	Jack Nicklaus	2001	Tiger Woods
1967	Gay Brewer	2002	Tiger Woods
1968	Bob Goalby	2003	Mike Weir

2004 Phil Mickelson
2005 Tiger Woods
2006 Phil Mickelson
2007 Zach Johnson
2008 Trevor Immelman
2009 Angel Cabrera

US Open Winners (PGA Tour golf – one of the four Majors)

1895	Horace Rawlins	1930	Bobby Jones
1896	James Foulis	1931	Billy Burke
1897	Joe Lloyd	1932	Gene Sarazen
1898	Fred Herd	1933	Johnny Goodman
1899	Willie Smith	1934	Olin Dutra
1900	Harry Vardon	1935	Sam Parks Jr.
1901	Willie Anderson	1936	Tony Manero
1902	Laurie Auchterlonie	1937	Ralph Guldahl
1903	Willie Anderson	1938	Ralph Guldahl
1904	Willie Anderson	1939	Byron Nelson
1905	Willie Anderson	1940	Lawson Little
1906	Alex Smith	1941	Craig Wood
1907	Alex Ross	1942	WW II
1908	Fred McLeod	1943	WW II
1909	George Sargent	1944	WW II
1910	Alex Smith	1945	WW II
1911	John McDermott	1946	Lloyd Mangrum
1912	John McDermott	1947	Lew Worsham
1913	Francis Ouimet	1948	Ben Hogan
1914	Walter Hagen	1949	Cary Middlecoff
1915	Jerome Travers	1950	Ben Hogan
1916	Charles Evans Jr.	1951	Ben Hogan
1917	WW I	1952	Julius Boros
1918	WW I	1953	Ben Hogan
1919	Walter Hagen	1954	Ed Furgol
1920	Edward Ray	1955	Jack Fleck
1921	James M. Barnes	1956	Cary Middlecoff
1922	Gene Sarazen	1957	Dick Mayer
1923	Bobby Jones	1958	Tommy Bolt
1924	Cyril Walker	1959	Billy Casper
1925	W MacFarlane	1960	Arnold Palmer
1926	Bobby Jones	1961	Gene Littler
1927	Tommy Armour	1962	Jack Nicklaus
1928	Johnny Farrell	1963	Julius Boros
1929	Bobby Jones	1964	Ken Venturi

1965 Gary Player
1966 Billy Casper
1967 Jack Nicklaus
1968 Lee Trevino
1969 Orville Moody
1970 Tony Jacklin
1971 Lee Trevino
1972 Jack Nicklaus
1973 Johnny Miller
1974 Hale Irwin
1975 Lou Graham
1976 Jerry Pate
1977 Hubert Green
1978 Andy North
1979 Hale Irwin
1980 Jack Nicklaus
1981 David Graham
1982 Tom Watson
1983 Larry Nelson
1984 Fuzzy Zoeller
1985 Andy North
1986 Ray Floyd
1987 Scott Simpson
1988 Curtis Strange
1989 Curtis Strange
1990 Hale Irwin
1991 Payne Stewart
1992 Tom Kite
1993 Lee Janzen
1994 Ernie Els
1995 Corey Pavin
1996 Steve Jones
1997 Ernie Els
1998 Lee Janzen
1999 Payne Stewart
2000 Tiger Woods
2001 Retief Goosen

2002 Tiger Woods
2003 Jim Furyk
2004 Retief Goosen
2005 Michael Campbell
2006 Geoff Ogilvy
2007 Angel Cabrera
2008 Tiger Woods
2009 Lucas Glover

British Open Winners (PGA Tour golf – one of the four Majors)

1860	Willie Park	1896	Harry Vardon
1861	Tom Morris Sr.	1897	Harold Hilton
1862	Tom Morris Sr.	1898	Harry Vardon
1863	Willie Park	1899	Harry Vardon
1864	Tom Morris Sr.	1900	J.H. Taylor
1865	Andrew Strath	1901	James Braid
1866	Willie Park	1902	Alexander Herd
1867	Tom Morris Sr.	1903	Harry Vardon
1868	Tom Morris Jr.	1904	Jack White
1869	Tom Morris Jr.	1905	James Braid
1870	Tom Morris Jr.	1906	James Braid
1871	N/A	1907	Arnaud Massy
1872	Tom Morris Jr.	1908	James Braid
1873	Tom Kidd	1909	J.H. Taylor
1874	Mungo Park	1910	James Braid
1875	Willie Park	1911	Harry Vardon
1876	Robert Martin	1912	Edward Ray
1877	Jamie Anderson	1913	J.H. Taylor
1878	Jamie Anderson	1914	Harry Vardon
1879	Jamie Anderson	1915	N/A
1880	Robert Ferguson	1916	N/A
1881	Robert Ferguson	1917	N/A
1882	Robert Ferguson	1918	N/A
1883	Willie Fernie	1919	N/A
1884	Jack Simpson	1920	George Duncan
1885	Bob Martin	1921	Jock Hutchison
1886	David Brown	1922	Walter Hagen
1887	Willie Park Jr.	1923	Arthur Havers
1888	Jack Burns	1924	Walter Hagen
1889	Willie Park Jr.	1925	James Barnes
1890	John Ball	1926	Robert Jones Jr.
1891	Hugh Kirkaldy	1927	Robert Jones Jr.
1892	Harold Hilton	1928	Walter Hagen
1893	William Auchterlonie	1929	Walter Hagen
1894	J.H. Taylor	1930	Robert Jones Jr.
1895	J.H. Taylor	1931	Tommy Armour

1932	Gene Sarazen	1969	Tony Jacklin
1933	Denny Shute	1970	Jack Nicklaus
1934	Henry Cotton	1971	Lee Trevino
1935	Alfred Perry	1972	Lee Trevino
1936	Alfred Padgham	1973	Tom Weiskopf
1937	Henry Cotton	1974	Gary Player
1938	R.A. Whitcombe	1975	Tom Watson
1939	Richard Burton	1976	Johnny Miller
1940	N/A	1977	Tom Watson
1941	N/A	1978	Jack Nicklaus
1942	N/A	1979	Seve Ballesteros
1943	N/A	1980	Tom Watson
1944	N/A	1981	Bill Rogers
1945	N/A	1982	Tom Watson
1946	Sam Snead	1983	Tom Watson
1947	Fred Daly	1984	Seve Ballesteros
1948	Henry Cotton	1985	Sandy Lyle
1949	Bobby Locke	1986	Greg Norman
1950	Bobby Locke	1987	Nick Faldo
1951	Max Faulkner	1988	Seve Ballesteros
1952	Bobby Locke	1989	Mark Calcavecchia
1953	Ben Hogan	1990	Nick Faldo
1954	Peter Thomson	1991	Ian Baker-Finch
1955	Peter Thomson	1992	Nick Faldo
1956	Peter Thomson	1993	Greg Norman
1957	Bobby Locke	1994	Nick Price
1958	Peter Thomson	1995	John Daly
1959	Gary Player	1996	Tom Lehman
1960	Kel Nagle	1997	Justin Leonard
1961	Arnold Palmer	1998	Mark O'Meara
1962	Arnold Palmer	1999	Paul Lawrie
1963	Bob Charles	2000	Tiger Woods
1964	Tony Lema	2001	David Duval
1965	Peter Thomson	2002	Ernie Els
1966	Jack Nicklaus	2003	Ben Curtis
1967	Roberto de Vicenzo	2004	Todd Hamilton
1968	Gary Player	2005	Tiger Woods

2006 Tiger Woods
2007 Padraig Harrington
2008 Padraig Harrington
2009 Stewart Cink

PGA Championship Winners (PGA Tour golf – one of the four Majors)

1916	James M. Barnes		1951	Sam Snead
1917	N/A		1952	Jim Turnesa
1918	N/A		1953	Walter Burkemo
1919	James M. Barnes		1954	Chick Harbert
1920	Jock Hutchison		1955	Doug Ford
1921	Walter Hagen		1956	Jack Burke
1922	Gene Sarazen		1957	Lionel Hebert
1923	Gene Sarazen		1958	Dow Finsterwald
1924	Walter Hagen		1959	Bob Rosburg
1925	Walter Hagen		1960	Jay Hebert
1926	Walter Hagen		1961	Jerry Barber
1927	Walter Hagen		1962	Gary Player
1928	Leo Diegel		1963	Jack Nicklaus
1929	Leo Diegel		1964	Bobby Nichols
1930	Tommy Armour		1965	Dave Marr
1931	Tom Creavy		1966	Al Geiberger
1932	Olin Dutra		1967	Don January
1933	Gene Sarazen		1968	Julius Boros
1934	Paul Runyan		1969	Ray Floyd
1935	Johnny Revolta		1970	Dave Stockton
1936	Denny Shute		1971	Jack Nicklaus
1937	Denny Shute		1972	Gary Player
1938	Paul Runyan		1973	Jack Nicklaus
1939	Henry Picard		1974	Lee Trevino
1940	Byron Nelson		1975	Jack Nicklaus
1941	Vic Ghezzi		1976	Dave Stockton
1942	Sam Snead		1977	Lanny Wadkins
1943	N/A		1978	John Mahaffey
1944	Bob Hamilton		1979	David Graham
1945	Byron Nelson		1980	Jack Nicklaus
1946	Ben Hogan		1981	Larry Nelson
1947	Jim Ferrier		1982	Raymond Floyd
1948	Ben Hogan		1983	Hal Sutton
1949	Sam Snead		1984	Lee Trevino
1950	Chandler Harper		1985	Hubert Green

1986 Bob Tway
1987 Larry Nelson
1988 Jeff Sluman
1989 Payne Stewart
1990 Wayne Grady
1991 John Daly
1992 Nick Price
1993 Paul Azinger
1994 Nick Price
1995 Steve Elkington
1996 Mark Brooks
1997 Davis Love III
1998 Vijay Singh
1999 Tiger Woods
2000 Tiger Woods
2001 David Toms
2002 Rich Beem
2003 Shaun Micheel
2004 Vijay Singh
2005 Phil Mickelson
2006 Tiger Woods
2007 Tiger Woods
2008 Padraig Harrington
2009 Y.E. Yang

NASCAR Winners

1949	Red Baron #22	1984	Terry Labonte #44
1950	Bill Rexford #60	1985	Darrell Waltrip #11
1951	Herb Thomas #92	1986	Dale Earnhardt #3
1952	Tim Flock #91	1987	Dale Earnhardt #3
1953	Herb Thomas #92	1988	Bill Elliott #9
1954	Lee Petty #42	1989	Rusty Wallace #27
1955	Tim Flock #300	1990	Dale Earnhardt #3
1956	Buck Baker #300B	1991	Dale Earnhardt #3
1957	Buck Baker #87	1992	Alan Kulwicki #7
1958	Lee Petty #42	1993	Dale Earnhardt #3
1959	Lee Petty #42	1994	Dale Earnhardt #3
1960	Rex White #4	1995	Jeff Gordon #24
1961	Ned Jarrett #11	1996	Terry Labonte #5
1962	Joe Weatherly #8	1997	Jeff Gordon #24
1963	Joe Weatherly #8	1998	Jeff Gordon #24
1964	Richard Petty #43	1999	Dale Jarrett #88
1965	Ned Jarrett #11	2000	Bobby Labonte #18
1966	David Pearson #6	2001	Jeff Gordon #24
1967	Richard Petty #43	2002	Tony Stewart #20
1968	David Pearson #17	2003	Matt Kenseth #17
1969	David Pearson #17	2004	Kurt Busch #97
1970	Bobby Isaac #71	2005	Tony Stewart #20
1971	Richard Petty #43	2006	Jimmie Johnson #48
1972	Richard Petty #43	2007	Jimmie Johnson #48
1973	Benny Parsons #72	2008	Jimmie Johnson #48
1974	Richard Petty #73		
1975	Richard Petty #43		
1976	Cale Yarborough #11		
1977	Cale Yarborough #11		
1978	Cale Yarborough #11		
1979	Richard Petty #43		
1980	Dale Earnhardt #2		
1981	Darrell Waltrip #11		
1982	Darrell Waltrip #11		
1983	Bobby Allison #22		

The End

www.ingramcontent.com/pod-product-compliance
Lightning Source LLC
Chambersburg PA
CBHW060349090426
42734CB00011B/2082